PHILOSOPHY

OF

TRINITARIAN DOCTRINE:

A CONTRIBUTION

TO

THEOLOGICAL PROGRESS AND REFORM

BY

REV. A. G. PEASE,

RUTLAND, VT.

NEW YORK:
G. P. PUTNAM'S SONS,
FOURTH AVE. AND 23D ST.
1875.

DEDICATION.

TO MY OLD ASSOCIATES IN THEOLOGICAL STUDY, AND IN THE LABORS OF THE CHRISTIAN MINISTRY, THIS LITTLE WORK, THE FIRST-FRUITS OF THE TOIL OF YEARS OF PHYSICAL PROSTRATION AND ENFORCED RETIREMENT AND SECLUSION, IS RESPECTFULLY AND AFFECTIONATELY DEDICATED.

If acquiescence without insight; if warmth without light; if an immunity from doubt given and guaranteed by a resolute ignorance; if the habit of taking for granted the words of a catechism, remembered or forgotten; if a mere sensation of positiveness substituted—I will not say for the sense of certainty, but for that calm assurance the very means and conditions of which it supersedes; if a belief that seeks the darkness and yet strikes no root, immovable as the limpet from the rock, and like the limpet fixed there by the mere force of adhesion;—if these suffice to make men Christians, in what sense could the Apostle affirm that believers receive: not indeed worldly wisdom, that comes to nought, but the wisdom of God, *that we might know and comprehend the things that are freely given us of God.* On what grounds could he denounce the sincerest fervor of spirit as defective where it does not likewise bring forth fruits in the understanding.—COLERIDGE.

The capital precept for the whole undertaking is this, that the eye of the mind be never taken off from things themselves, but receive their images truly as they are. And God forbid that ever we should offer the dreams of fancy for a model of the world; but rather in his kindness vouchsafe to us the means of writing a revelation and true vision of the traces and moulds of the Creator in his creatures.—BACON.

PREFACE.

THE term Trinitarian, in the title of this work, is intended, not to imply a discussion of the doctrine of the Trinity exclusively, but rather to indicate the point of view from which the topics here presented, and indeed the whole circle of Christian doctrine, have been contemplated by the writer. He was originally led into the train of meditation, some fruits of which are now submitted, by a desire and effort to learn by inquiry of the Scriptures themselves what is the purely Scriptural doctrine of the Trinity. The view which there unfolded itself to him of the person of Christ and His relation to the Father and to Humanity, not only appeared intelligible and consistent with itself, in marked contrast to those which the current theological standards afforded, but also became, with increasing study, more and more evident as the central parent luminary of the whole system of theological truth, the life-principle out of which it all grows, as the branches out of the Vine; as "all the building, fitly framed together, groweth into an holy temple in the Lord" out of "Jesus Christ Himself the chief corner stone." Divine philosophy, as thus revealed, is indeed something manifestly different from the formularies commonly accepted as orthodox; but the writer trusts that it will appear to some other minds, as it does to his own, thoroughly in harmony with the one Catholic faith which the constructors of those formularies aimed to crystallize in shapes of logic, with how imperfect success, the holiest and wisest of them have been readiest to acknowledge. Of course the contents of this little work constitutes no more than a mere beginning, and comes very far short of covering the whole of the ground indicated by the title. In fact my own studies and labors have taken a much wider range and include a much larger outline and a much fuller and more systematic treatment than appears or is even indicated in this volume. They include such leading topics as the following, which, to atone in some measure for the extremely incomplete and fragmentary character of this publication, may be briefly indicated :

General conception of the creation as an organic Unity, and of the organic relation existing between God and the universe according to Aristotle, and in fact the clearly taught philosophy of the Scriptures themselves ; the Godhead itself an organic Unity within itself ; distinction of rank and power—of greater and less—of the universal and the particular among its elements essential to the existence of any such thing as an organic Unity or a Trinity comprehended within it ; the idea of the Trinity unfolded and the doctrine stated ; the nature and person of Christ.

The relation which Christ sustains to men in the manhood analogous to and explained by the relation which the Father sustains to the Son in the Godhead ; the principle of the power and perpetuity of Christianity found in the example of Christ as God manifest in the flesh ; Christ as our atonement ; the office work of the Holy Spirit, as illustrated by Scripture and by natural and Platonic symbols and analogies ; the doctrine of original sin—sin an altogether inorganic and individual affair in opposition to the Augustinian theory of the organic unity of the race in sin ; the organic unity of mind in the universe, including the Eternal mind as the principle of unity ; the source and foundation of law and of ethics ; ante-Nicene history of the doctrine of the Trinity, showing the prevalence of the subordination theory among the early Greek fathers ; intellectual life, freedom, and progress, as affected by the Nicene Council ; the doctrine of the Trinity, as illustrated and taught by analogies from Plato and from nature ; miracles ; faith, and reason ; the trinity of principles in the constitution and life of the soul, and in the life of the church—a lively image of the Trinity of persons in the Godhead. *And now abideth Faith, Hope, Charity, these three ; but the greatest of these is Charity. I and my Father are one, but my Father is greater than I.* The ideal state of Plato and the Christian church of Paul compared. A. G. P.

RUTLAND, *Dec.* 8, 1874.

CONTENTS.

PHILOSOPHY

OF

TRINITARIAN DOCTRINE.

I.

The philosophical and religious necessity of the organic conception of the world and of the Deity.

THE failure to recognize the organic unity of the Godhead, and the regarding it instead as an abstract unity, has been the fruitful source of error and mischief in theology, and many a fatal stumbling-block has been thrown in the way of a rational faith in Christianity by means of it. The truth is, that God cannot be known at all, or be a real object of knowledge or of thought to any mind, except by means of his organic nature and connections with the universe. If he has no organic connections; if he is to be regarded as absolutely one and simple—without any organic relation of parts or elements within

2

himself, or any organic relations with anything outside of himself—then there are no means by which he can be known at all. By the very supposition he has no attributes, he is a subject without properties—a thing, therefore, that cannot be known, simply because it has no real objective existence, but is a mere form of thought, a mere abstract conception without any corresponding reality in nature. Aristotle says, *there can be no such thing as a science of the unique.* By the unique, he means that which is absolutely one and simple in itself, and destitute of all organic connection with anything outside of itself. It is obvious that that which is within itself thus inorganic—not a unity but a mere unit of abstraction—can have no external connections or means of connecting itself with external things either as cause or effect, either as antecedent or consequent.

Of course, there can be no science of any such thing, for it has no contents and no attributes, and is therefore, objectively speaking, a nonentity. It is merely a conception of the mind, not corresponding to anything objectively real, but standing only as the subjective opposite to reality. If God is unique, that is, absolutely one and simple in his nature, then he has no attributes; and if he has no attributes he is objectively nothing. He has no connections with things outside of himself by means of which he can be known, no means by which he can reveal himself to us. Even if he were supposed to have a reality, an actual nature of his own, he must have known attributes, or else he cannot reveal himself. The revelation cannot be direct and immediate. The subject can be known only by means of its known properties. The cause only by means of the effects which it produces. If known at all, it must be through the medium of some result flowing from it, or effect which it produces. We can know nothing of causes but from their effects. The reality of the cause is inferred from the reality of its effects and the nature of the cause from the nature of the effects. But if a cause has no organic connections with things outside of itself, it can produce no effects upon those things—there is no way by which it can act upon things with which it has no connection. We can be directly conscious only of ourselves—of the operations of our own minds, or of effects and impressions made upon our minds. If we are to have consciousness of God therefore, it must be through the medium of our self-consciousness, or through the medium of impressions of which we are conscious, and which we find ourselves obliged to refer to him as their source. But God cannot in this way enter into our consciousness unless there exist organic connections between his mind and ours. How can the mind of God enter into our minds, and we, through the consciousness of our minds, know his mind, unless there is an organic connection between his mind and ours? If we are to know his mind at all, it must be as it makes itself known to us in our minds. God reveals himself *to* us, that is, makes known to us his being and his attributes only as he reveals himself in us and *through* us. But in order that he may reveal himself *through* us, he must himself be *in* us. But this he can be only vitally and organically. There is no way by which he can be said to be in us, except by means of his life. Only that which is itself life can enter into life. Only lives and living forces can inter-penetrate each other and dwell within each other, thus forming an organic unity of life within life, mind within mind. If mind were not living it could not enter into mind, and form by their mutual indwelling and inter-penetration an organic unity of mind. His mind cannot be organically one with our minds, except by being the *mind* of *our minds*—or the universal principle of mind within our particular minds, by means of which the real nature and life of mind is imparted to our minds, and we become rational and living souls. We can have one life with God only as his life becomes the life of our lives. If he is not *far* from every one of us, it is because he is actually within us. By the *not far* is not meant a short distance from us in space—a slight remove externally from us—but that he is within and not without us at all, whether far or near. The *far* relates to that which is without—the *near* to that which is within. If in him we live, and move, and have our being, it is not mechanically nor figuratively, but vitally and organically. I have said that if God has no organic connections—is not organically connected with any being that is not his own—then he has, properly speaking, no attributes. If his mind is a distinct and separate individuality, complete in itself, and acting separately and independently of anything in vital relations with it, then he has no attributes—none, at all events, which we have any means of knowing anything about, or of forming any conception of; but it is only by means of his attributes that we can have any knowledge of him. The attributes of a cause are the same thing to us as its nature. They are to us the expression of its nature, or the particular aspects and qualities by which it makes itself known to us. As, for example, good, wise, just, great, and their contraries. A moral and intellectual cause of which none of these can be predicated, has for us no nature or character, and if without nature, or intellectual or moral qualities, it is nothing to us. The attributes or qualities of a cause, whether physical or moral, are known only by the nature of the effects which it produces. Its nature as a cause—that is, the kind of cause or being it is—can be known only by the kind of effects which it produces.

A good tree bringeth forth good fruit, and an evil tree evil fruit, the tree is known by its fruit.

If the effects of which we are conscious within ourselves, or which come within our observation or experience, whether within us or without us, whether intellectual and moral or external and physical, and which by the necessary laws of thought we ascribe to God as their cause, are what we recognize as *good*, then on the ground of these effects, we ascribe goodness to God. We say that none but a good being could have produced them. If another class of effects which likewise we ascribe to God exhibit wisdom, a clear comprehension of ends to be gained and the best means of gaining them; if we see means adapted to ends in such a way as to indicate the profoundest and most consummate and far-seeing wisdom, we cannot avoid having the conviction fastened upon us by these manifestations, that the being who could devise and carry out such a system of things, and accomplish such ends by such means, must be endowed with infinite wisdom. This we do on the principle that the tree is known by its fruit. Again, if we find ourselves so constituted—our inner being so made up—that we instinctively take the highest delight in justice, and cannot but rejoice and be glad when we see justice done, and its ends gained, and its enemies overwhelmed, and if we find the universe, so far as we are acquainted with it, constructed upon the plan and with the evident design of establishing justice, and of having its kingdom come, and its will done throughout the rational and responsible creation, the conclusion to which we are inevitably brought, and which becomes as certain to us as the fact of the creation itself, is that the author of the universe, and the Father of our spirits in whom we and all things live, and move, and have our being, is an infinitely just being.

It is thus through his organic connections, that God reveals his nature and his attributes to us. A cause that produces no effects—a cause that cannot be studied in its effects—a cause whose attributes are not in reality seen in its effects,—is not a cause—and a cause that is not a cause is nothing. But every cause that is a cause, lives and moves and has its being in its effects, and its effects live and move and have their being in it. Thus there is no such thing as life or being that is unique, there is none that is not organic; there is none that has not in it at the same time the nature, and that does not discharge the double function of cause and effect. Thus all life and being are dualistic—there is nothing that is unique. There are unities indeed, and in fact nothing but unities, but these unities are at the same time Dyads. There is not in nature such a thing as a monad. We can think monads; not as objective realities, however, but only as their subjective contraries. Unity in the abstract is a thing of the mind—it has nominal and notional reality merely. But every real object which we can call a unity is concrete, and consists of correlate forces or elements in organic relation to each other.

The unity of the Godhead implies its *duality*—special revelation adds another element and makes known to us the Trinity. But in principle, the Dyad is a philosophical necessity; and the unity of the being of God is not a thing conceivable or possible except as involving organic relations within itself and organic connections with the universe which forms his counterpart. Cause and effect are counterparts and correlates. The one cannot exist or be conceived as an objective reality except as existing with the other, and with it forming an organic unity. Causes as such never stand in immediate relation to us. We know them only through their effects, or through the manner in which we are affected by them. Effects as such, are known to us immediately. They are the direct and immediate matter of our consciousness. We know them in themselves, but their causes only in and by means of them.

Thus we do not *a priori* assume the goodness of God, and from that reason to the effects which he produces, and say, these must be so or so because he is such or such. We do not judge of the character of the effects which he produces by what we know *a priori* of his character. We do not point to the acknowledged effects, and say these must be good because he is good. We do not judge of the fruit from the tree, but *a posteriori* of the tree by its fruit.

We do not upon *a priori* grounds (if there are any such grounds) assume the justice of God, and then say that what he does is just because he is just and cannot act any other way than justly, and *therefore whatsoever he does is just because he does it.* That would be simply to judge of the just and the unjust in character and conduct, without any idea of the nature of justice in our minds as our standard or criterion of judgment. To judge of the nature of effects from the assumed nature of their cause, would be to say that effects have no nature or character of their own; that justice is arbitrary, depending upon will and prescription, and that our opinion of the justice of an act depends upon nothing inherent in the act itself, but upon the opinion we entertain of the character of him that performs it.

We have only (for example) to make the will of a despot the standard of right and wrong, and such a thing as unjust government, or as oppression and cruelty in a ruler, becomes impossible.

But taking the nature of our own consciences and the instinctive verdict of our moral sense as the standard, judging, that is, by the standard of nature and conscience within our own souls, and perceiving the goodness and righteousness of the effects which we refer to him as their cause, we are obliged by the necessary laws of thought to infer the goodness and justice of the being who produced them. From the effects as revealed to us in our own consciousness, we necessarily infer a cause adequate to their production; from the *nature* of the effects, as judged of by our own moral sense, we infer the *nature* of the cause. We do not assume the goodness of the tree and thence pronounce upon the nature of the fruit which it must bear. We do not say of a given species of fruit, this fruit must be good because the tree which produced it is a good tree, or of another sort, this fruit must be evil—there is no need of tasting or trying it in order to determine whether it is good or not. That point is already determined *a priori* for us by the nature of the tree, from sources independent entirely of any fruit it bears; it has been proved to be a good tree; of course being such, the fruit which it produces, whatever it may be, as judged of by our tastes, or its effects on us, must be good. In order to determine the nature of a fruit, and determine whether it is good or not, we have but one question to ask, and that is, what sort of a tree is it which has produced it? Now if we had the means (as absolutely we have not) of judging of the nature of the tree on grounds wholly independent of the fruit it produces, this would be good reasoning. It is true that a tree which is good can produce none but good fruit. But what means have we of determining the nature of a fruit-tree but the nature of the fruit it bears? None, whatever; the tree, then, is to be known by its fruit, and not *vice versa*, and the nature of the fruit is to be determined by actual trial and experience of the effects resulting, and the pleasure or disgust experienced in eating it.

The character of the fruit-bearing and tree-producing principle in the tree, can be known only by the tree into which it develops itself, and the fruit which that tree produces. The character of the moving cause can be determined only from the character of the final cause.

If a cause by its working produces only that which is evil, we have a right to infer, if it is intelligent, that it wrought only for the sake of producing evil. If it works intelligently and produces only evil by its working, we have a right to impute to it evil *motives*, and that which in working is actuated by evil motives, or thê end of whose working is evil, is an evil cause. If a tree bore no fruit, it would have no character as a fruit-tree. Indeed, it would not be a fruit-tree at all. So, of a cause which produced no effects we should have no means of judging at all. In fact, it would not be a cause at all, and not being a cause, it would be nothing.

But suppose your so-called cause, or fruit-bearing principle, were strictly and solely a simple and separate thing, and had no organic nature or connections—in other words, were an abstract and absolute unit—that is to say, a monad and not a dyad—what then? Why, then there could be no such thing as its development into a tree or organic body, and of course no such thing as its bearing fruit, or producing effects. A monad cannot be a fruit-bearing nor even a life principle. It cannot be developed into anything; as it came from nothing, so nothing can ever come from it. It can have no means of making itself known as anything whatever, from the simple fact that, as a monad, it is, objectively speaking, *nothing* whatever. So if the life-principle of a tree were a monad, with no organic nature or connections whatsoever, if it could not develop itself into a tree, having root, trunk, branches, and leaves, it would certainly be incapable of bearing fruit. If, then, the tree is known by its fruit, and if without organic nature and connections—if, except as it develops itself into a tree, it is impossible that it should bear any fruit, or produce any effects at all, then there is no way in which the principle of a fruit-bearing tree, or the nature or fact of a cause, can be known but by means of its organic nature and connections. As the fruit-bearing principle of a tree therefore is known only through its organic connections, that is, through its connection with the parts, members, and organs of the tree into which it develops itself, or which it builds up to serve as its body, and as a habitation and means of manifestation for itself—as without reference to its organic connections the principle of life in a tree is a thing unknowable and inconceivable by us—so, also, is it impossible for us to have any conception whatever of God, if we insist on conceiving of him as a simple individual inorganic existence, without reference to the organic relations which he sustains to the universe. For it is only by means of his relations to the universe, as its organic principle and fountain-head, that it is possible for us to have any knowledge or idea of him at all. And it is only in virtue of his relations to the universe as its living cause that he has, as a cause, any character, any attributes, any nature at all. As it is only by means of its relation to its branches, that is, to its organic connections, that it is possible for us to have any knowledge of *the vine*, and as it is only in relation to the nature of the branches which it produces that the vine has any attributes or character at all, so it is as to God and his attributes, and our knowledge of him. There is the same necessity of conceiving of him in his organic relations, in order that we may know anything of him or he be anything to us, as there is in the case of the vine.

The being, the life, and the attributes of God the Father, the fountain-head and life-principle of the Godhead, make themselves known in the person and attributes of the Son. Just as the life, nature, and attributes of the vine make themselves known in the nature and the life of the branches. The life of the vine has two correlative and counterpart elements—the vine or root-element, and the branch-element. Together these two elements constitute the organic unity of the life of the vine as an organic whole.

As such a whole it must be known, and must exist, or it cannot be known or exist at all. In the branch, the life of the vine is developed—goes forth into act and visibility. The attributes and the character of the Father are seen in the life of the Son. *The life of the Father manifests itself in the life of the Son. The life of the Son is the living product of the indwelling life of the Father.*

Just as Christ lives and reveals his character and attributes in the life of the church, which is his *body*, the manifestation and the measure of that life of his which filleth all in all, and the life of the church, is the product of the indwelling life of Christ, who is its fountain-head. "*As the living Father hath sent me and I live by the Father, even so he that eateth me even he shall live by me.*" The Son lives by the Father just as the church lives by the Son. Whilst at the same time the lives of the Father and of the Son are not one and the same, but each has a distinct and peculiar life of his own; and the church and its Head have not a single life in common, but each has a life of its own, distinct but not separate, from that of the other. The attributes of the Father and the Son are not identical any more than their lives, whilst at the same time it is only in and by means of the Son that the attributes of the Father can be revealed. The attributes of the Father may be *in* those of the Son without thereby becoming his. They remain the same, and his own, the same as though they were not embodied and expressed in another life organically (but not hypostatically) one with his.

The attributes of Christ reveal themselves in his body the church; but they do not thereby become its attributes, so that he and it having the same attributes are one and the same thing. Absolute, independent, self-existence is an essential attribute of the life of the Father, distinguishing it from the life of the Son, which is not absolutely self-existent, but as Christ himself expressly says, *I live by the Father!* But the Father is "*living*" in the absolute sense, that is, in the sense of living *by* himself and not *by any* other. His life flows from nothing, has no original, no source, no fountain. Being itself ultimate, and the absolute and unoriginated life, it becomes the life-principle and fountain-head of the life of the Godhead and of the whole creation. The Son is indeed the immediate fountain-head of the life of the creation—*all things were made by him and without him was not anything made that was made*—but the life of the Father is fountain-head to that of the Son, and so ultimately and absolutely to that of the whole creation. The life of the Son is the immediate source of the life of the creation.

The life of the Father is in the life of the creation, but not immediately, but only in and through the life of the Son. The life of the Son mediates between that of the Father and that of the creation. The life of the Father is not separated from that of the universe, but is in it, yet only mediately, through the life of the Son, so that the life of the Father, and of the Son, and of the creation, taken together, constitute that grand organic unity of life which comprehends all the life there is, and all that ever was or ever can be life or being at all.

Suppose now that instead of this organic unity of life constituted by the life of the Godhead, and of the creation, the being of God were conceived of as a something standing outside and independent of all organic connection with our being. Suppose his being and nature to be a thing apart from ours, and sustaining only an external and mechanical relation to that of the universe, and a thing of which we can have no knowledge by means of our own inward life and experience. Suppose him to stand entirely outside of all possible creaturely experience and consciousness, what knowledge is it possible for us to have of him? What possible or conceivable means have we of knowing anything about him? Is it answered that we may know him by means of his works?

But what means have we of recognizing anything as a work of his, or of connecting him with any work as its author? Effects do indeed presuppose causes, but there is nothing in any natural effect to throw any light upon the nature of its cause, except as that effect involves in its own nature something of the nature of that cause. Spinoza most truthfully and profoundly says, that if two things have nothing in common, the one *cannot be the cause of the other.* If then the cause be not within the effect, there can be nothing in the effect from which we can obtain any knowledge of its cause. For example, if there is nothing of God of which we can be conscious in our actual experience, then there is nothing in our experience to throw any light upon the nature or character of the source from which our natures sprang.

The fact is, that we do instinctively and necessarily in obedience to the logic of thought refer all that we see in nature, and all that is actual and living in our own experience or in the universe to a cause within, and not external and mechanically or arbitrarily related to, itself. We do not when following the natural laws of thought go outside of the universe to find somewhere within the domain of infinite space something to which we may ascribe it as its cause. It does not seem to us possible, that there can be any such separation between the cause and the effect—between the fountain and the stream that flows from it. Nay, we know that no such separation exists. We know that it belongs to the nature of things that stream and fountain should stand in immediate relation to each other. That two things cannot sustain to each other the relation of stream and fountain, if the one is externally separate and foreign from the other. And cause in the organic creation means, not force acting externally to produce its effects, but life and living energy working inwardly and organically. If God were not internally and vitally connected with the universe as its cause, there would be nothing in it from which we could infer anything in regard to his nature or attributes.

In the grand and comprehensive similitude of the vine and its branches, by which Christ sets forth the relation between himself and his people (or his normal relations to humanity), he also indicates the relation which exists between himself and the universe. It is not necessary to confine the illustration to the narrower relation which exists between him and the souls of regenerate men. We may extend it to the whole universe of being, and say, precisely as the vine is related to its branches, so is God related to the universe. As Christ, in the special relation to the souls of his people, is vine; so God in the universal relation and as universal creator is vine to the universe. All that we mean to include under the term universe, comes, according to the illustration, under the general head of branches. And all which there is within the universe, which we yet distinguish from the universe, is represented by the term vine. Thus the organic unity of God and the universe is exactly represented by the similitude of the unity of the vine and its branches. If we do not *(e. g.)* look outside of a tree for the source of the branches, if the invariable and universal instinct of thought teaches us to look *inside* of a tree for the source of its branches, so the natural logic of our minds teaches us that the principle of the life and the unity of the universe must be within the universe and not somewhere or somehow outside of it. We do not, under the leading of the instinctive tendencies of our minds, go about seeking outside of the creation for the creator, outside of "the things that are made" for the power that made them.

Nothing but the creation indeed, can lead us to the knowledge of its author. It does lead us to such knowledge; and the whole end for which it exists is to lead to it, but it points us to what is within, and not to something, we know not what, lying somewhere, we know not where, outside of itself, for the knowledge which we seek, for the source from which it springs. Through all its living species, and all its cosmic harmonies, through all its ranks and orders, it says to us, if you would know the life of the Creator—if you would know what manner of life it is which he lives, seek the knowledge of it in our lives, *for he lives in us.*

Such, therefore, as our lives are in their principle, such also is his life—for in him we live and move and have our being—his life is the principle of our lives—*it is our lives in their principle.* The life of God and the life of nature are not one and the same life, but the life of nature is the living product of the life of God, and his life produces and sustains the life of nature, and establishes and maintains the order and the unity and the harmony of the universe—not as something existing extraneously to it, and operating upon it from without as external and mechanical will and force, but by living and exerting his own vital energies within it. Out of this circle thus pervaded by the life of God, it is impossible for us even in thought to pass; for there is outside of it nothing for thought to fasten itself upon, and therefore nothing that it can pass to; and there would be no means of making the passage or of bridging the chasm between that and us, and thus reaching the other side, if there were another side to it. For life can be joined to life only by living links, and there is no chain by which the living cause can bind its effects to itself, but one whose links are living, and forged out of the material of its own life.

In the realm of mechanism, the cause does not live and move and have its being in its effects, nor (*vice versa*) do effects live in the life of their causes, and therefore there is nothing in the effect to reveal anything in relation to its cause, except force and skill sufficient to contrive and produce it. All that a watch, for example, reveals in reference to its maker is, that he, for some reason or other, wanted an instrument by which to measure time, and that he had power and skill enough to contrive and manufacture this. Nothing more than this can be known about his purposes or his ends, his faculties or his character, if we are limited to the watch as our source of information. Let us not then allow ourselves to be referred any more to a cause outside of the universe, and sustaining only mechanical relations to it, to explain the mystery of its nature or the fact of its existence. It exists *from* a cause and *for* a cause within itself. And it is, and is what it is, because that cause is, and is where and what it is. It could not have existed at all except *from* a cause—and it could not have been what it is, except for a cause influencing the mind of him who produced it. And the cause that has produced such a universe as this must have possessed the height of wisdom and intelligence, and been actuated by motives of infinite goodness and love.

How beautifully and conclusively the apostle treats this argument in his address to the Athenians on Mars' Hill: *Forasmuch then*, he says, *as we are rational and intelligent beings, capable of proposing* to ourselves the wisest, the noblest, and best ends in all that we do, and never consciously acting without motives or without reference to an end, *we ought not to think that our Creator is like unto silver or gold or stone, graven by art and man's device.* He teaches them that it is a logical absurdity, as well as inconsistent with anything like a rational religion, to think that our Creator is so utterly unlike us and so immeasurably inferior to us as that makes him. He teaches that to ascribe life, reason, intelligence, moral and intellectual faculties, religion and love, as we find them in ourselves, to dead, senseless inorganic matter—mere metal and stone—as their cause—is as contrary to reason and common sense as anything can be, and the grossest imposition and wrong that we can practice upon ourselves, unutterably degrading to our humanity, and demoralizing to our natures.

Thus it is wholly owing to the organic relation

existing between God and the universe, that it is possible to obtain any knowledge of him by means of it, or that it throws any light upon the question of his nature or his attributes. When I say that nature points within herself for the explanation of the fact of her existence, and says, if you would know the secret of my origin seek it within me, she does not mean to refer her origin to herself, and to say that she is her own creator; but that the principle out of which her life and being have flowed, is, (*not herself, but*) *within herself*,—and works and manifests itself in and through her. She means to bear witness to the organic connection existing between herself and her divine original. Not that the two existences and natures are one and the same thing, identically, but that they are organically one, the one existing within, and as the producing cause and fountain-head of the other.

God lives in nature and nature in God, that they may be made perfect in and by virtue of their organic unity. Does not Christ recognize this great principle of the organic relation between nature and God, when he prays in words not otherwise intelligible, that they all *may be one, as thou Father art in me and I in thee, that they also may be one in us. And the glory which thou gavest me I have given them, that they may be one even as we are one,*

I in them and thou in me, that they may be made perfect in one.

Thus much for the relation between God and the universe, and for the manner in which God is made known to us, and we arrive at the knowledge of him through the medium of his works. If they were not organically connected with him,—he in them and they in him,—there would be nothing in them to throw light upon the question of his nature, or to impart any knowledge or idea of him. If God were not within his work and within us, the idea of God as it is reflected upon us from the things which he has made, and especially in the light of our own inward being and consciousness, could never have had being in our minds. Just as external objects are to us what they reveal themselves to be through our bodily sensations and experience; as external experience is our only source of knowledge regarding them, so is our inward experience the only source of any true knowledge concerning God. He only that knows something experimentally of the soul's life and of the life of God in the soul, knows anything of God at all. He alone has proper and trustworthy conceptions of the nature and attributes of him that made him. All that comes to us from other and outside sources, and is not the reflection of the light and of the witness of the spirit within, can be little else than *vain wisdom* all, and *false philosophy.* It can be little else than superstition and folly, and an imposition upon our ignorance, our weakness, our fears, and our credulity. If we receive what we call the knowledge of God from any source but the Spirit itself, witnessing in and with our spirit, what we receive must be falsehood, whose only tendency is to quench the inward light, to put out the eye and destroy the life of our souls. Except as with the eye of our own spiritual being we "read the eternal deep"—and in our inward experience are conscious of the presence of something within us that is infinite, all holy and Eternal—and thus, to use the language of Wordsworth, of being "haunted forever by *the Eternal mind*," it is impossible that that mind should be revealed to us. The greatest foe to human progress and elevation, the greatest obstacle in the way of the true knowledge of God, is a material and mechanical philosophy which has usurped the place of reason and experience, and the laws of spiritual life, in the interpretation of nature and of the Scriptures, and in the construction of our theological systems. There can be no such thing as genuine and radical reform in our theology, and we can never arrive at a true interpretation of nature and Scripture without a reformed philosophy, in the place of the arbitrary and lifeless systems that have so long held almost undisputed and unquestioned sway; which know nothing of any force but that which is materialistic, and recognize no laws of nature but those of mechanical action and reaction, and no life of nature but what is the result of them.

What is needed is a philosophy that recognizes nothing as real, or entitled to any place in the nature of things, but what is living and organic, that acknowledges no universe but the living universe, no God but the living God; no relation between the universe and God, but that between the living body and its living Head, between the living and the life-giving vine and its living branches.

But our argument is incomplete until it has done more than to prove the necessity of the organic connection between God and his creatures, in order that they may have the means of any right knowledge of him. It must prove, also, the organic unity of the Creator within himself. It must demonstrate the philosophical and religious necessity of conceiving of the Godhead as an organic unity, and not as unique, or absolutely one and simple in the nature of its being, and without organic connection to anything that has living being outside of itself.

Between God and a monad there is nothing in

common, and no resemblance—none whatever. God has living and organic relations, as has been proved; but a monad, according to its definition, has no such relations, and it belongs to the necessary conception of it that it should have none. Therefore, God is not a monad. If not a monad, or *abstract unity*, then, if he is a unity at all (and he is a unity), he must be an organic unity.

Whatever, then, may be the nature or the intimacy of the relations between God and us, the divine nature and ours are not the same. The Godhead has a nature of its own, distinct and different from that of the *manhood* (or the Humanity considered as an order of being); the two orders differ not in degree or rank merely, but also in kind. The one nature does not differ from the other merely as a different form or modification of a nature which at bottom and essentially is one and the same. The Creator cannot change his own essential form and nature and become a creature. *God cannot become a man, any more than a man can become God.* When we speak of God and a man we are uniformly understood to be speaking, not of two different modifications of one and the same nature, but of two different natures—the one that of the creature, the other that of the creator. Now, how is the one, the creature-nature, to come into vital union and experimental and conscious communion with the other, the creator-nature, differing as the two natures do, not in degree merely, but also in kind? It is only in virtue of those elements which the two natures have in common; it is only, that is, in virtue of the *communion* of nature between two persons, that the one can, with his consciousness, enter into the consciousness of the other, so as thus to become conscious of the consciousness or of the feelings of the other. Such interpenetration of experiences requires a common nature, so far, at least, as these correlated and counterpart experiences are concerned.

How, then, can the mind of man come to the experimental knowledge of the mind of the Godhead? (For we know the Godhead only in so far as we know its mind, or know it *in* its mind.)

The doctrine of the organic unity of the Godhead gives the only possible answer to that question. The conception of the Godhead, as an organic unity, furnishes the only answer, and reveals the only means by which the two natures can be brought into fellowship and communion of feeling and of knowledge with each other. *There is one God and one Mediator between God and man (that is, between the Godhead and the manhood), the God-man Christ Jesus.* The mind of the Godhead reveals and communicates itself to the mind of man through the mediation of the nature and person of Christ, who is at once and in his *one nature,* both God and man. The two natures meet and combine in the one undivided and indivisible nature of the man Christ Jesus—who is man in the sense of being not *a man,* but the principle of our humanity—or our humanity in its principle. Now, between Christ and us there is communion of nature, because he is our nature in its principle, and surely there can be no obstacle to the most vital and intimate communion of knowledge and feeling between each individual man, and him who is not a man, but the very life and life-principle of all that is human in his nature. But if he combines in his one nature the two natures—the nature of the Godhead and that of the manhood, thus in communing with him (as we are enabled immediately to do through his real humanity), we commune with the nature and heart and mind of the Godhead through him. Not directly with the Father, because between his particular nature and ours there is nothing in common, but our communion is with the Father indirectly through our communion with the Son.

Christ, through his divine nature, and as himself within the Godhead, is in immediate communion with the Father. There is no necessity of a mediator between him and his Father, any more than there is of a mediator between us and Christ. There is an organic unity of life and of nature between the Father and the Son, so that in communing with him we are brought, through the medium of his life and nature, into communion with the life of the Father, which is in him as the life-principle of his life. (John vi. 57.) This mystery is plainly asserted by Christ himself. He admits the impossibility of any immediate knowledge of the Father by us; but at the same time says, that having seen him, we are without excuse if we say that we have not seen the Father. He that hath seen me hath seen the Father. How, then, after having seen me, sayest thou, "*Show us the Father?*" Believest thou not that I am in the Father, and *the Father in me?* The words that I speak to you I speak not of myself, but the Father that *dwelleth in me—he doeth the works.* Believe me that I am in the Father, and *the Father in me.* Hence, Christ being organically one with us, and at the same time organically one with the Father, brings our nature into organic relations with the Supreme Deity of the Father. It is thus by means of the organic relations of the Godhead within itself that it becomes capable of entering into organic relations with us, and thus of communicating himself vitally and intelligibly to us.

In order that the nature of Christ may mediate between the nature of the Father and our nature, his nature must in some respect be different from ours at the same time that it is one with it. If it were in no respect different from ours, it could not stand as a *third term between ours and another nature.* His occupying a position between the two parties makes it necessary to regard him as being in some sense one with both, at the same time that there are respects in which he differs from both. If in his own proper and peculiar nature he did not combine properties of the nature of both, the two could not meet in him, and he could not be the medium, and mediate between them. If, besides, there were not respects in which he differs from both, he could not be reckoned as a third term or party between them. In what respect, then, is Christ one with us? I answer, he is one with us as being *not one of us, but all of us, and all there is of us,* except our *imperfections and our sins.* In other words, he is one with us as being our humanity in its principle and fountain-head. He and we are one, to use his own illustration, in the sense that the vine and its branches are one, and he differs from us as the vine differs from the branches. *I am the vine, ye are the branches.* The vine and its branches are not so one but that the vine has a life of its own, distinct and different from that of its branches, whilst the branches have a life of their own distinct and different from that of the vine. To make the matter plain, and show clearly and beyond the need of any possible mistake, how it is that the Son mediates between the Father and us, we have only to represent Christ by the vine and ourselves by the branches, thus showing at once the oneness and the difference between him and us. Then, suppose that the vine is itself branch to something else which is to it what it is to us. Let Christ thus be represented as standing between his Father, who is his vine on the one hand, and us, who are his branches, on the other, and the illustration is complete. He mediates between the Father and us by being at once branch to him and vine to us. He is in his Father and his Father in him, just as we are in him and he in us. If it were not, then, for the organic relations existing within the Godhead—if it were not at once within the unity of its own being both Father and Son, it could sustain no organic relations to us, and without these there would be no means by which we could come to the knowledge of it. *

* To show that in what I have written entirely "without book," and on the sole authority of Scripture and my own mind, on this fundamental point of the mediatorial nature of Christ as God-man, medi-

ator; that only as being both God and man could he mediate between God and man, but that whilst uniting the elements of both parties in his one undivided and indivisible nature he must be different from both in order not to be identical with either party, but to constitute a third party standing between the two; I say, in order to show that on this great point, though trusting to myself under no leading but that of the plain and necessary sense of Scripture, I have not shot very wide of the mark of the free and unsophisticated judgment and opinion of the best minds of the best age of the Christian Church, I desire to add here the admirable statement by Neander of the position of the great Athanasius, firmly and consistently maintained by him in the Nicene Council, and, amidst all the changes, strifes and persecutions that resulted immediately from it, never departed from by him. The statement of Neander reads like a grand summing-up and condensation of all the vital points concerned in the great controversy so fraught with results and consequences of weal and of woe, but especially of the latter, to the Church in all the succeeding ages.

"After having been enlisted but for a short period in favor of the Homo-onsion he (Constantine) had been drawn back again to those earlier views, which would so much more readily present themselves to a layman contemplating the matter simply in its outward aspects, that personal passions and a self-willed, disputatious spirit had given to these questions, which did not pertain in the least to the essentials of Christianity, an undue importance. The Emperor entertaining this view of the matter, all who agreed in representing the doctrinal differences as unimportant, would especially commend themselves to his favor; while all who were unwilling, for the sake of gratifying the Emperor, to moderate their zeal in behalf of a truth which they found to be intimately connected with the essence of Christianity, would easily become suspected and hated by him, as uneasy, contentious and disorderly men.

"Hence may be explained the contests which first and prëeminently the remarkable person had to pass through who had now become the head of the Homo-onsion party in the Eastern Church. For soon after the conclusion of the Council of Nice, the bishop Alexander had died, and was succeeded by the archdeacon Athanasius, a man far his superior in intellect and resolute energy. Athanasius had probably been already, up to this time, the soul of the party in favor of the Homo-onsion, and it was by his influence that the bishop Alexander had been led to decide that nothing should be yielded in order to the restoration of Arius. Moreover, he had already distinguished himself at the Nicene Council, by the zeal and acuteness with which he defended the doctrine of the unity of essence, and combated Arianism. By pursuing with strict consistency and unwavering firmness, during an active life of nearly half a century, and amid every variety of fortune and many persecutions and sufferings, the same object, in opposition to those parties whose doctrinal views were either unsettled in themselves, or liable to veer about with every change of the air at Court, he contributed in a great measure to promote the victory of the Homo-onsion in the Eastern Church. If we consider the connection of thought and ideas in the doctrinal system of this father, we shall doubtless be led to see, that, in contending for the Homo-onsion, he by no means contended for a mere speculative formula, standing in no manner of connection with what constitutes the essence of Christianity; that, in this controversy, it was by no means a barely dialectic or speculative interest that actuated him, but in reality an essentially Christian interest. On the holding fast to the Homo-onsion depended, in his view, the whole unity of the Christian consciousness of God, the completeness of the revelation of God in Christ, the reality of the redemption which Christ wrought, and of the communion with God restored by him to man. 'If Christ,' so argued Athanasius against the Arian doctrine, 'differed from other creatures simply as being the only creature immediately produced by God, then he could not bring the creature into fellowship with God, since we must be constrained to conceive of something still intermediate between him, as a creature, and the divine essence which differed from him, something whereby *he* might stand in communion with God; and this intermediate being would be precisely the Son of God in the proper sense. In analyzing the conception of God communicated to the creature it would be necessary to arrive at the conception of *that which requires nothing intermediate in order to communion with God; which does not participate in God's essence as something foreign from itself, but which is itself the self-communicating essence of God.* This is the only Son of God, the only being who can be so called in the proper sense. The expressions Son of God and divine generation are of a symbolical nature, and denote simply the communication of the divine essence.

It is only on the supposition that Christ is, in this sense alone, the proper Son of God, that he can make rational creatures Children of God. It is the Logos who imparts himself to them, dwells within them, and through whom they live in God—the Son of God within them, through the fellowship of whom they become themselves Children of God.' It is here seen how in Athanasius the idea of the Homo-onsion presented itself in connection with what constitutes the root and groundwork of the entire Christian life. While the Arians mantained that it was impossible to distinguish the conceptions Son of God and generation from God from the conceptions *created being, and a creature,* without falling into sensuous, anthropomorphic representations, Athanasius on the contrary, taught that all human expressions of God were of a symbolic nature, taken from temporal things, and therefore liable to be misconceived unless the idea lying at the bottom were freed from the elements of time and sense, *and the same attribute,* predicated of God, understood in a different manner from what it would be when predicated of creatures. Even God's act of creation, in order not to be misconceived, must be distinguished from the human mode of producing and forming. As the Arians admitted that, according to John v. 23, divine worship belonged to Christ, Athanasius accused them of showing that honor to a creature, according to their notions of Christ, which belonged to God alone; consequently of falling into idolatry. From this coherence of the doctrines which Athanasius defended with his whole Christian consciousness, it may be well conceived that he must have considered himself bound by his duty as a pastor, not to admit into his Church a teacher who held forth a system which appeared to him to be so thoroughly unchristian."—*Neander's History of the Christian Religion and Church.* Vol. II., pp. 380, 381.

II.

Christ, the Principle of our Immortality.

THE prevailing doctrine respecting our immortality is, and has for the most part been, that the soul is naturally and essentially immortal; that the life imparted to it at its creation is a thing that having once been must forever be; that it is dependent on nothing outside of itself for sustenance or support, but is in such a sense self-supporting that no withdrawal of the favor or the support of its Creator on the one hand, nor any inflictions of his anger on the other, can in the least affect the strength of its hold on life, or the conditions upon which the perpetuity of its existence depends. This doctrine, of course, denies the existence of any organic connections between the life of the soul and the lives of other living beings in the universe. It makes it a poor, finite, solitary, inorganic object in the abyss of infinite being, living necessarily, twinkling endlessly, in spite of itself, and in spite of all assaults of finite evil, and all withdrawal of divine support, living by the inherent necessity of its own nature. This is not only the pagan doctrine, but, strange to say, the prevalent Christian doctrine, notwithstanding that it finds no support in Scripture, and is contrary to reason and to the analogy of nature and of Christianity.

But the Christian history shows that the first shining of the light of the Gospel had a strong tendency to cast doubt on this view of the subject. As matter of fact, Justin Martyr,* who was bred a Platonist, and the first of the Christian fathers whose writings are extant, was led, as soon as he became a convert to the Christian faith, to deny the Platonic doctrine of the natural and inherent immortality of the soul, as directly and radically inconsistent not only with the analogy of Christianity, but with the plain and express teachings of Christ and His apostles. Many of the early Greek fathers of the ante-Nicene period agreed with him in this opinion, and it was the prevailing sentiment of the educated Christian mind of the first three centuries. Justin understood Christ tacitly to deny the inherent and natural immortality of the soul, and to ascribe it to Himself as its eternal principle, and to teach that it could belong to man only as derived from the absolute source, the Eternal Father, through him. Christ represents himself as

* He sealed his testimony with his blood in the persecution under the Emperor Marcus Aurelius.

the bread of immortality which came down from heaven, that a man may eat thereof and *not die*, which is as much as directly to say that there is no principle of immortality in man by nature, and that if he does not derive the principle (the bread) of it from Christ, there is nothing to prevent his dying as the brute dies. He further says: *Except ye eat the flesh and drink the blood of the Son of Man ye have no life in you*—that is, nothing that survives the body, nothing that exempts you from the same death that overtakes and destroys forever all the successive ranks and generations of animal as well as vegetable life that swarm on all the face of the earth. The Apostle John puts this point in a very strong light in several unequivocal passages, which I cannot forbear quoting in this connection. *And the world passeth away and the lust thereof, but he that doeth the will of God abideth forever.* What fair and unforced interpretation can be put upon these words by those who hold that immortality is irrespective of character, that the wicked are immortal, and as certain of *abiding forever* as the righteous! Again, this same apostle says: And this is the record: that God hath given to us eternal life (that is, immortality), and *this life is in his Son*—he that hath the Son hath immortal life, but he that hath not the Son hath not life. It is only, that is to say, by having the Son that we can have the life of which he is the principle. The commonly-received doctrine, however, denies this dependence of the soul for its immortality upon a vital and spiritual union with Christ, and makes it a matter of nature and necessity, and insists upon the immortality of the soul as a thing entirely independent of character, or any relations which the soul may sustain to the spirit and life of Christ. It makes it a separate, inalienable, necessary possession, depending wholly upon nature and not at all upon grace, and belonging to the worst as well as to the best of men; to those that are out of Christ, and cut off from the life of God by the wickedness which is in them, as well as to those that are in Christ and drink most deeply into the spirit of his life, and draw most abundantly from him the life of their lives. But no man can, in view of the cardinal facts in the case, be rationally persuaded of the truth of any such doctrine of immortality as this. What support can it find, either in Scripture or reason, experience or analogy? We say none: there is no evidence of its truth; on the contrary, all nature, reason, Scripture, and analogy, are against it. Men have held to it for lack of Scripture light, and because they have not understood the philosophy of life and of living nature.

It is, in short, because they have not learnt that great and fundamental principle of nature which all fact supports, without a solitary known or conceivable exception—*that all life is organic;* that there is not anywhere in the world, either of nature or spirit, any such thing as a life that is *unique*—or absolutely one and simple, individual and solitary—with no organic connections within itself or with any other life. The truth is (and the proposition needs only to be made in order to secure universal assent), that life exists in species, races, and orders, and in no other way: beneath the throne of God there is not such a thing as life that does not belong to a living species. And, moreover, there is no such thing as a species that does not constitute an organic unity, consisting of its fountain-head and its members—of the universal generic principle of unity and of life, and of the particular members with their individualizing and differentiating characteristics which receive their unity and their generic character from it. It is impossible that there should be any such thing as life in an individual which he does not derive from the life-principle or fountain-head of the species to which he belongs. For he cannot exist without being either himself the generic principle of a species, or belonging to a species as a particular member of it—

just as it is impossible that there should be life in a branch which is not derived from the vine with which it is in living and organic connection. Accordingly, Christ represents it to be wholly owing to our organic connection with him that we have any power to bear fruit, or even to live at all--as the branch cannot bear *fruit of itself* except it abide in the vine. And as to the possibility of our living without vital connection with him, he says, *Without me ye can do nothing*—you cannot even so much as live, or be at all, to say nothing of the ability to bear fruit. If a man abide not in me, he is cast forth as a branch that has separated itself from the vine (supposing such a thing to be possible), and men gather them and cast them into the fire, and they are burned. We do therefore greatly err and involve ourselves in great and needless darkness and distress of mind, in reference to this great question of our immortality, when in thought we isolate ourselves from all organic connection with the eternal fountain of life, and strive to believe in our immortality—in a life that survives the wreck of the grave and the doom of all merely natural things and perpetuates itself to all eternity. For it is not upon an individual status, nor in our individual capacity without reference to our organic connection with the great whole of the body, and the great principle of the body's life, that we are to regard the question of our immortality. It is not an individual so much as an organic question. The question is in reality in reference to the immortality of the organization to which we belong, and of which we are living and essential members and organs. If that is immortal, we are immortal. Our destiny is bound up with that of the system of which we are members, and of which we constitute essential and organic parts. If that lives, we shall live. Accordingly, Christ speaking of himself as the fountain of the body which is his church, says, *Because I live ye shall live also.* The body cannot die so long as its head lives, and no member of that body, whose life is thus assured, can die so long as it remains a member, and retains its vital connection with the organic source and principle of life.

To individualize ourselves, and look upon ourselves in our merely individual capacity without reference to the body or organization to which our souls belong, and strive to believe in our immortality on such a false assumption as that, is like striving to believe in the continued and perpetual burning of the flame of a lamp without reference to the oil in the lamp, from which it is fed. It is as though we should expect the flame to burn on forever without any lamp, or any oil in the lamp to feed and sustain it. The flame must have something to draw upon besides itself before it can have any chance to burn for any great length of time. It requires more than an individual supply. It must have the lamp beneath it, and the supply in the lamp must be inexhaustible enough to support the innumerable flames on the particular burners that branch out from it. If we are to have the true faith of our immortality, the faith *that is full of immortality and full of glory*—that undoubting and blessed assurance which is the privilege of the Christian, we must look upon ourselves not in our individual capacity, but as one with all the redeemed in Christ Jesus. We never have any difficulty in embracing with perfect assurance the immortality of our Lord Jesus Christ. Indeed we cannot help believing in it, for he is not *immortal*, so much as immortality—the principle itself. We cannot, therefore, believe in him without believing in immortality so far as concerns him. But to believe in it *as it is in him* is to believe in it also in regard to those that are in him, for they cannot die whilst he lives unless they shall separate themselves from him or be separated from him against their wills. But neither of these is possible. There is no power that can separate us from the love and the life of Christ—so long as we love him, and having loved him once it is impossible to conceive of the possibility of the voluntary withdrawal of our love.

What Christ is he must forever be, and what he has he must forever keep. My sheep hear my voice, and I know them, and they follow me: and *I give unto them eternal life, and they shall never perish; neither shall any pluck them out of my hand.* My Father which gave them me is greater than all, and no man is able to pluck them out of my Father's hands. Moreover, with the same assurance with which we believe in the immortality of Christ, we believe in the immortality of the church, not merely as an organization that is to be perpetuated, but in the immortality of each of its members. For in that organization it is not necessary that one generation of its members should die and pass away in order to give place for another. Its generations do not die. Nay, it has no succession of generations as the species in nature have, but all its members from the first to the last constitute but a *single generation.* There is *increase* but *no succession.* The one generation of believers in Christ is not born till we all come, from the first to the last believer, *in the unity of the faith and of the knowledge of the Son of God unto a perfect manhood—unto the measure of the stature of the fullness of Christ.*

But what is the ground of this implicit faith which

we have in the immortality of the church? It is that it is the church of the living God. It is that we know that its head is a living head, and the unconscious and necessary ratiocination of our minds in the premises is, that because he lives, she shall live also. The church lives because it is inseparable from its living head. It lives and it must live because he, who cannot die, whose grand distinction is that *he ever liveth*, lives in it, to maintain its life, and to cause it to flourish in undecaying youth and vigor forever. If the source of the life of *his body* were mortal, as the principle of our bodily life is, then *his body* would die just as ours does. If the life-principle of our bodies were immortal as that of the body of Christ is, then our bodies would be immortal as his body, which is the church, is. What, then, have we to do in order to be fully and finally established in the doctrine of our individual and personal immortality? I answer, we must habitually and in obedience to the spontaneous and natural logic of our feelings and our instincts regard ourselves, not in our individual, but in our organic capacity, not as standing each alone, as a single stalk on its own separate root, but as members of his body, and rooted and grounded in him who is the one root and life principle of our humanity. Nothing else can do so much for us because nothing else is so true to nature, or puts us at the true point of view in reference to this great subject, as this view of our organic relations to Christ, our common membership and fellowship with each other in his body does. The radical principle upon which this argument rests, and which is to be steadily kept in view, is *that the life of the body implies the life of its members. The member that is separated from the body instantly dies. The member that abides and keeps its place and performs its functions in the body lives as surely and as long as that lives.*

This holds universally; as regards the members of the natural body—the hand, the foot, the eye, the ear—its truth is self-evident; and as soon as it is stated and the attention called to it, it is vividly impressed upon the mind, as representing the universal and most fundamental principle within the realm of the natural life. There is life for the member only in the place where it grew, only in the place where and for which it was produced. When it is no longer what and where nature made it to be, and when it no longer answers the end or performs the function for which nature made it, *it is nothing*. It annihilates itself by removing itself out of its organic connections. Out of and independent of these connections it can *do* nothing and it can *be* nothing. It is in reality nothing, when it is not what it was made to be, nor doing what it was made to do. In these its natural relations, it has not only its usefulness, its honor, and its prosperity but its *very being* also. Only ask again what becomes of the branch when once it is severed from the vine, and the connection which made it organically one with the vine cut off. What is there for it but to perish; and what is there that can save it from death? Nothing! There is no power in heaven or earth, in God or man, whereby the life of a branch thus severed from all vital connection can be preserved in life. God and nature can act only in conformity with their own laws of action and of being. It is not in the power of miracle to make such a thing as that severed branch live. No such miracle ever was wrought or ever can be. There is no help for such a branch, no, not in nature nor in miracle.

Now the only question is whether this principle does not hold and apply equally and in all its force within this spiritual realm! Is not *all life organic*, the life of the soul as universally and necessarily as that of the body? Whatever may be the differences between the life of the soul and the body they are exactly alike in this, that they are both and equally *organic*. And it is just as impossible for a soul to exist, or be anything out of its organic relations as it is for a member of the natural body, or a branch of the literal vine. Christ establishes this beyond a peradventure by illustrating the conditions upon which the life of the soul depends, by the comparison which he draws from physical nature. If the analogy and the law of nature in this respect did not extend to, and were not uniform and identical through, the two realms there would be no force in the comparison. Nothing could be learned by it. What he intended to teach would not be taught, viz.: that *all life is organic*, life in the realm of spirit, equally with that in the realm of physical nature.

He intends to say: the relations which your lives sustain to mine are organic, your lives sprang out of mine and are dependent on mine, just as much as that of the branches springs out of the vine and is dependent on it. Out of me and of organic relation with me, life is no more possible for you than for the branch that is cut or broken off from the vine. Other Scriptural symbols teach the same thing, as, notably, that in Eph. iv. 15, 16, where the relation between the church and its head is illustrated by the relation which the animal body sustains to the life-principle out of which it grows. See also Eph. ii. 21, 22.

Now if this be so, if the soul has no more a life of its own independent of its life-principle and organic head than the branch a life of its own independent of the vine in which it lives and out of which it grows; then how can the result of organic separation be different in the one case from what it is in the other? The Saviour himself expressly says there is no difference, that the result in both cases is the same. And that for the simple reason that the soul has no more a life that is unique and independent of organic connections than a branch of a vine or a member of an animal body. To the soul, therefore, that separates itself from Christ, its spiritual head, there is no more possibility of life than there is for a branch that is separated from the stock on which it grew.

In the one case, it is true, the separation is voluntary, in the other not. But that makes no difference as to the result, which must in both cases be the same, *and that is death!*

It is within the option of the spiritual branch to say whether it will separate itself or not; but it is not within its option to determine whether, after the separation it will remain a living thing, a living soul, or not! That is a question that is determined for it by the law of its nature and of its creation and which is not left for it to settle for itself. Separated from the source of life, cut off from the eternal fountain-head from which all life springs, how, thus unfueled and unfed, is it going to perpetuate its life? Can it become a life-source for itself? Is there any such potency in its freedom of will as to enable it to accomplish this more than miracle—this greater wonder than any that God himself can perform for it? Can it in the might of its own innate and inherent freedom, in its being's separation and exile, accomplish it for itself? Can it in its own strength perform for itself what God cannot by any strength which he possesses perform for it?

Can it change its nature, and its rank, and its office, in the scale of being at its own pleasure, and from being a branch become at once a vine, an organic principle and life-source, the source of life not only to itself, but to others also? If it cannot do this, then, if it is to exist at all, it must remain just what, and just where, God made it to be. If he made it for a member or an organ of some other life which is fountain-head to it, then such it must remain, or be nothing. But separated from the Living Spirit from which it grew, and of whose life it is the product, it cannot perform the functions of an organ. The Spirit can no longer dwell in it, and use it as its organ when it is no longer a part of its body, and stands no longer in any vital relations with itself. When it is no longer one of the constituent elements, or parts that from the indwelling of the the living corner-stone are organized together into an holy temple in the Lord—into an habitation of God through the Spirit, it will be nothing at all—it will have no being when it has no place in, and constitutes no part of, the living temple. Not being in the Lord, nor the Lord, it is impossible to conceive what it can be, or how it can be at all. It becomes a thing without a life, without a nature, without a relation, without a function. It is neither cause nor effect—it is neither antecedent nor consequent—it is neither subject nor object—it is neither root or branch, body or spirit, property or subject. It is a thing *unknown*, *indefinable*, *unknowable*, *inconceivable*, and *impossible!* Existence is inconceivable upon such terms and under such conditions. The attempt to state what it is, is simply the statement of the impossibility of there being any such thing at all. Why, then, ascribe not only existence, but immortality, to a thing of which none but a negative description is possible.

The problem it presents is, *Given negative properties without number, out of their joint action to produce a positive subject.*

There is no such thing as creaturely life that has not its root in the eternal and absolute life of God. And the Divine life itself exists not alone. There is, indeed, no other life on which it depends, and out of which it springs, but it has branches growing out of it, inseparable from it, and dependent on it. But the problem which the existence of the soul that has alienated itself from the life of God through the wickedness which is in it, and loved darkness rather than light because its deeds are evil, is how to maintain an inorganic and absolutely separate life, dependent on no other and with no other dependent on that. The consequence to the soul by placing itself in such a position as that, if position it can be called, is not life, but death—not the exchange of one character for another merely, nor of one condition or situation of life for another, but of life for death. This result follows not merely from the character of God, nor from the principles of the Divine administration, except as those principles are identical with the organic structure and constitution of the universe. The universe is so made, its fundamental principles and laws are such, that a question of administration resolves itself into a question of essential constitution and the eternal and unalterable nature of things. The universe is so made, then, that the natural and inevitable consequence of sin unrepented of—of sin carried to a point beyond the possibility of forgiveness—is to sever the vital connection between the source of the life, which in its nature is immortal, and the soul; and such a severance, according to the universal and unalterable laws of organic life, can result in nothing but what the Scriptures call "*death*." The soul has no alternative. It must maintain its normal relations with the life of God, or it must perish. For God so loved the world that he gave his only begotten Son, that he that believeth in him might not perish, but have a life which is everlasting. Nothing can be everlasting, *nothing in the universe of God lasts forever but holiness*. There is no everlasting life of evil, of misery and sin. It is unalterably ordained among the fundamental and primal decrees of the Divine Government that nothing which in its nature is evil, and which is productive of nothing but misery, shall be perpetual. Only that whose nature is good, and whose only result is happiness and unalloyed well-being, shall last forever. If its nature be evil, its hold on life is temporary and transient—only the life which is love is happiness and true well-being; and therefore, the life of love is the only one that has any promise or possibility of an endless continuance. Accordingly, we have the law and the constitution laid down in words that admit of no doubtful construction. The wages—*the natural and inevitable and guilty consequence of sin unrepented of and unforgiven is death: but immortal life and everlasting blessedness are the gift of God through Jesus Christ our Lord.* And St. James gives the genesis, the growth, and final result of sin. He recognizes the *fact*, and describes the nature and the origin of sin; but he denies the *perpetuity* of a thing having such a nature and parentage as that. He says: Every man, when he is tempted, is drawn away by his own *lust and enticed. Then, when lust hath conceived it bringeth forth sin, and sin, when it is finished, bringeth forth death.* Sin is a thing that is some time or other to have an end, and it is a thing that in finishing itself, completing its work, and arriving at its maturity, finishes its subject. It lives upon him, and lives in him, as long as there is anything in him for it to live upon, and then it dies, and he upon whom, and in whom it has fed and lived, of necessity dies with it. He dies because the vital forces within him are all destroyed, and his vitality all *consumed;* and the consumption of vitality in this case must mean not the consumption of the vital principle, but the sundering of his connection with it through the gradually corrupting and destroying power of sin in his soul. Gal. vi. 8. And this is no novelty either in doctrine or interpretation. It has always been the implicit and the practical faith of the sincere believer, whether he has thought the matter out and intelligently accepted it in theory or not. Let Coleridge, under the inspiration of the truth as well as of his own genius, express the true faith of our immortality for us :

God's child in Christ adopted, Christ my all ;
  What that earth boasts were not lost cheaply, rather
Them forfeit that blest name, by which I call
  The holy one, the Almighty God, my Father !
Father, in Christ we live, and Christ in thee,
Eternal thou, and everlasting we.
The heir of Heaven, henceforth I fear not death,
In Christ I live ; in Christ I draw the breath
Of the true life. Let then earth, sea and sky
  Make war upon me, on my heart I show
Their mighty master's seal. In vain they try
  To end my life, that can but end its woe.
Is that a death-bed, where a Christian lies ?
Yes ; but not his. 'Tis death itself there dies.

And, furthermore, in the plainest prose he declares the same doctrine, which is the implicit and real, though for the most part suppressed doctrine of the church universal, that immortality is not an inherent attribute of the human soul, so that whatever may be its character or condition it must still live ; but that it is the gift of God, through Jesus

Christ, our Lord. In the Aids to Reflection (Introductory Aphorism XIII.), he says: "Never did there exist a full faith in the Divine Word (by which light, *as well as Immortality*, was brought into the world), which did not expand the intellect while it purified the heart, which did not multiply the aims and objects of the understanding, while it fixed and simplified those of the desires and passions."

III.

Actual personal relations between the Father and the Son, and subordination in rank of the Son to the Father—(the Son equally with the Father within the Unity of the Godhead, but not equal with him in it), as set forth in express terms by Christ himself.

An Exposition of John v. 8–20.

THIS exposition is given for the purpose of showing how perfectly real and practical the personal relations between him and his Father were to Christ, and how he claimed to exercise divine power and prerogatives equally with his Father, at the same time that he is equally careful to represent himself as acting and standing in a subordinate relation to him within the Godhead.

It has been customary with Trinitarians to deny that the relations between the Father and the Son in the Godhead are strictly personal or even intelligible in their nature. They say that there is a distinction, but insist that it is *sui generis*, that it is like no other relation that comes within our knowledge, and that consequently there are no analogies or means by which we can form any conception of what it is. All we can know of it is *that* it is. The term "personal" they say is used to describe it for want of a better, not because it is really such. But that of which we can have no conception is, and must forever be, nothing as a matter of knowledge to us. In asking us to believe in the doctrine, therefore, they say that they do not themselves know what it is in which they ask us to believe. They ask us to believe in the Trinity as a fact of which no explanation can be given. But it is not an explanation that we ask for, but only the privilege of being informed what the fact is in which we are required to believe. A rational explanation is not necessary in all cases in order to a rational faith, but that we should have some intelligible idea of what that is in which we profess to believe is necessary. We cannot rationally say that we believe in what is expressed in a formula of words unless we know what it is that the formula expresses, or, at least, that it expresses *something* besides obvious absurdity and self-contradiction.

Christ, however, treats the distinction as a thing not only real, but intelligible. He compares himself with his Father in office, in power, in working—mind with mind—heart with heart—exactly as though it were a matter between parent and child, or one man and another, and there is no good reason why he should not be understood accordingly. It is certainly most unreasonable to undertake to shape his utterances to correspond with such utter darkness and confusion as reigns in the orthodox statements of the doctrine of the Trinity and of the person of Christ.

The matter with which the passage before us opens, though upon another subject, is not irrelevant to the general subject of this work. For including it, therefore, I make no apology, especially as it stands in such close internal connection with the main topic.

John v. 8, 9—"*Jesus saith unto him, rise and take up thy bed and walk. And immediately the man was made whole, and took up his bed and walked, and the same day was the Sabbath.*"

This scene of healing seems to have been no more than an ordinary instance of the exercise of that miraculous power which was his by nature, and his to exercise at his own will and pleasure. Our English word "walk" seems not to be the exact equivalent of the corresponding word in the originals, which means literally, "to walk about at pleasure." Our phrase, "go about your business," would come nearer to it. The meaning then is: You need no longer lie here; go where your business or your inclination calls you. He spoke, and though it was the Sabbath, and the man knew that it was not lawful for him to carry his bed on that day, yet he obeys without question or hesitation, seeming to recognize the presence and authority of a higher law, in the command of him who had made him whole.

The same day was the Sabbath. It was obviously on account of this circumstance chiefly that this miracle is here recorded. For of the innumerable miracles which he wrought John records but very few, and those having a marked character and specially pertinent to the purpose of his gospel. It was not that his conduct in this instance was at all singular, or out of the ordinary course as regarded his treatment of the Sabbath. For it was not. But in this instance special notice was taken of his conduct, and it gave rise to that remarkable discourse respecting his divinity and his relations to the Father, which John was specially desirous to reproduce and introduce into his record.

Jesus was quite as likely to work miracles on the Sabbath as on other days. Indeed, so far as his life and work were concerned, he made no difference among the days. But the days were not all alike to the Jews. They put a marked and radical difference between them. Hence the unavoidable collision, and the bitter war they waged against him. Not on this ground only. The ground was general; but this uncanonical treatment of the Sabbath was used as the most prominent specification under the general accusation of disregard to the law of Moses.

10. *The Jews, therefore, said to him that was cured, It is not lawful for thee to carry thy bed.*

He was observed carrying his bed—"a mere pallet, which, when rolled up, made a bundle no bigger or heavier than a soldier's overcoat." Yet that made no difference. Big or little, light or heavy, it was a burden, and must not be borne. "A Jew might play on the Sabbath, join a social festivity, grow hilarious, but he must not work."

11. *He answered them: He that made me whole, the same said unto me, take up thy bed and walk.*

He could not think obedience to the command of him who had shown such power and goodness could be a sin. It could appear no otherwise to him than as a duty, notwithstanding it was a breach of a Mosaic statute. He thought that one who had thus proved himself the Lord of nature must be Lord also of the Sabbath day.

The Jews seem tacitly to have admitted the force of the argument so far as the man was concerned, that in a measure, at least, it furnished an excuse for his conduct, even if it did not fully justify it. But they saw in it no excuse for Jesus. For what had he been guilty of doing? He had been guilty of a twofold and most aggravated breach of the law. He had not only broken the Sabbath himself by needlessly performing a cure on that day, but he had caused it to be broken by another person when there was no need of it. He might have waited until after the Sabbath before performing the cure, and the man, though cured, might have waited until the next day before carrying his bed. But Jesus, it seems, saw no reason why the man should not be cured on that day, although it was the Sabbath, nor why, being cured, he should not use the health and the strength that had been conferred upon him as soon as it was conferred. The power was given to be used and enjoyed on all days alike. In fact, there was no violation of any divine law in the case either by Jesus or the man. In the presence of Jesus, and in the face of his work and his word, there was no Sabbath. The institution was virtually abolished.* Then and there and thenceforth it ex-

* The Lord's day and the Jewish Sabbath are not to be confounded. The one is observed in commemoration of the resurrection of Christ on the *first* day of the week, and is necessary for the purposes of rest from worldly toil, and Christian worship, edification, and comfort. The other is an element of the system of Jewish types and shadows, which, having been fulfilled in Christ, has passed away. Matt. v. 17, 18.

isted only in the minds of the Jews. In the mind of Jesus it had ceased to exist as authoritative over the consciences or the conduct of men, after he, the Lord of the Sabbath, had come to displace the shadow and replace it with the substance, which substance He, himself, was. Compare Col. ii. 14–17; also Rom. xiv. 5, 6.

15, 16. *The man departed and told the Jews that it was Jesus that had made him whole. And therefore did the Jews persecute Jesus, and sought to slay him, because he had done these things on the Sabbath day.*

17. *But Jesus answered them: My Father worketh hitherto and I* (also) *work* (in imitation of his example).

He is not an observer of days nor of seasons, so neither am I; as he knows no Sabbath in the prosecution of his work, so neither do I in the prosecution of mine. The Sabbath was not made for him, neither was it made for me. I am as independent of it in my work as he is in his.

18. *Therefore the Jews sought the more to kill him, because he not only had broken the Sabbath, but said also that God was his Father,* (thus) *making himself equal with God.*

The defense which Jesus had made, so far from justifying him in their view, seemed only an aggravation of the original offense, or seeking to justify one sin by the commission of another and a greater one. To justify his breach of the Sabbath, he commits (say they) the crime of blasphemy against God. He does, indeed, whether it be blasphemy or not, claim equality with God, so far at least, as this; that he equally with him is free from the obligations of the Jewish Sabbath, and that it is just as absurd for them to think of imposing it upon him, expecting him to regulate his conduct by it as it would be to think of imposing it upon God with the expectation that his work in nature and in providence would be regulated by it. He thus gives them distinctly to understand that he is as much above the jurisdiction and authority of their Sabbath as God himself is. That it is just as absurd and will prove to be quite as much in vain for them to throw the barrier of their Sabbath across the path of his working and his will, as it would be for them to forbid the sun to shine, and require nature to pause in her operations and do no work on that day.

19. *Then answered Jesus, and said unto them, Verily, verily, I say unto you, the Son can do nothing of himself but what he seeth the Father do, for what things soever he doeth these also doeth the Son likewise.*

The undercurrent of thought must be clearly

apprehended, the interior link of connection must be perceived, or these words will be dark and enigmatical to us, and criticism and explanation will be expended on them in vain. What, then, is the clue to the meaning of this verse? I answer, the Jews had charged him with making assumptions with regard to himself that were in the highest degree presumptuous and dishonorable to the Divine Majesty, with arrogating to himself divine honors and prerogatives. For to say that God was his Father, what was it but making himself equal with God? And what was that to them but blasphemy, repudiating as they did his claim of a Divine nature and origin? "That thou being a man makest thyself equal with God," was the charge which they brought against him, (chap. x. 33). Now the elucidations which he gives on the great and awful theme of the personal relations between the Father and the Son in the Godhead, have reference in the particular form in which he puts them in this place to the false conceptions of those to whom they were addressed. He means that they shall know, if by words he can make them understand it, just how far they are right and how far wrong in saying that he had, by what He had said, made himself equal with God. He wished them to understand that if he had claimed equality with God, the nature of the equality intended was such as involved no dishonor to God, no blasphemy, nor any unwarrantable pretensions on his part. He wished to make it plain to them that the equality which he claimed was not inconsistent with a real subordination on his part to the person and dignity of his Father, and, therefore, in his answer he proceeds at once to make known the fact of his subordination and dependence, notwithstanding that he did the very same things and in substantially the same way in which his Father did them. His statement in the 17th verse, was that in working he imitated his Father. He now proceeds to explain this—to show how he can work just as he does and do the very same things, and at the same time be subordinate to him in respect to inherent original power, dignity, and will. *Verily I say unto you, the Son can do nothing of himself.* He means that though he is really and truly God, that though he is of the substance of the Godhead, he is not the fountain-head of that organic unity of life and being which is called by that name—that whatever exists in him existed first in the order of nature in his Father, as the fountain-head of life, power, wisdom, will and authority in the Godhead—that whatever he is or knows or does is by derivation from him who is the life-principle and fountain-head even of the Godhead itself. What he means, then, by saying that the Son can do nothing of himself, is, that though his works are his own, and in that sense truly original, yet they do not proceed from him as the original and ultimate source of life, power and wisdom. That in the absolute sense—in the sense of original underived wisdom and power—it is the Father that dwelleth in him that doeth the works. He says expressly that he works by imitation and example—that neither his ideas nor his power are original with him. He gives us plainly to understand that in the absolute sense he originates nothing, and is not himself original, but that his Father is the original of both himself and his works. He represents his works as a copy or image of the Father's only inasmuch as they were the works of him who is himself the image of the invisible God. His works are, therefore, in this sense imitations; they are images of those of the Father.

What then is this? To be able himself to do whatsoever he has seen the Father do, and to work perfectly in the idea and spirit of that paternal mind? This power of perfect universal comprehension, insight and imitation of the infinite and Eternal

Original—does any creature or any finite being possess it? No, the original itself is not further beyond finite knowledge and power than such imitation. The Father himself is not more completely beyond finite power and imitation than is the Son in what he understands and does. And what, on the other hand, is this? Not to be able to do anything until he has first seen it in his Father? To be able of himself to originate nothing—to do nothing of which he has not first seen the original and the example in his Father? I say, what is this but subordination and dependence? And then to complete the representation, he adds most impressively, as it seems to us (20th),—*For the Father loveth the Son and showeth him all things He himself doeth.*

His view of the example and working of his Father is not a narrow, partial, or imperfect one. It extends over the entire field, and there is nothing so minute as to be beneath his notice or to escape his observation; nothing so vast or so profound as to be beyond his easy comprehension and his perfect knowledge. He knows it as well as if he had himself been its immediate author, and the idea and the plan of it had been the product of his own mind. He enters with infinite ease into the uttermost depths of the divine mind and the divine agency as revealed in the particular works, and understands each work not merely as it is in itself, as an effect, but as it is in the cause out of which it springs.

Whatever in the mind of the Father exists in idea merely, comes forth out of the mind of the Son as a realized ideal. The Father loveth the Son for this reason, because of this perfect insight which he has into the designs and workings of his own mind, and the perfect ability he has of carrying them out into overt acts, and realizing them in actual works, which, when he looks upon them, fill his heart with satisfaction and delight, and he pronounces them to be all very *good.* They are *good* to him, because they perfectly correspond to his own ideal, fully answer his design and accomplish his purpose ; and, besides, they seem all the more beautiful and good to him because they are the handiwork of his only-begotten and well-beloved Son.

The Father loveth the Son because he is the perfect medium through which his own ideas find their expression, and he loveth his own works all the more for the sake of the beloved medium through which they are all wrought. This delight which he feels in having his own ideas thus perfectly realized, his own wishes thus perfectly fulfilled, causes him to love the Son all the more, and to *show him all things which himself doeth.*

This apprehensive and imitative faculty of the Son, this power which he possesses of converting the eternal ideas into actual, concrete, living realities, is exactly commensurate with the divine ideals, and with the originative wisdom, power, and goodness of the Father.

In the form of expression which he uses to set forth his own divine nature, and to assert the right which he has to claim divine honors without derogation of the rights of his Father, there is what, for the want of a better name, we may call a divine modesty.

His Father, he says, loves him so entirely that he confides everything to him, conceals *nothing* from him, opens his inmost heart fully out to him, and showeth him all things which himself doeth.

See how, with a certain innate modesty and shrinking from self-praise, he speaks when asserting his own divine claims in comparison with those of his Father. He prefers magnifying the Father's love rather than his own divine greatness. But it is on account of this inherent greatness of the Son, in which he has no fellow, as well as on account of the Father's love to him, that all things are thus shown to him. They could not, indeed, be shown to any one else, because no one else would be capable of appreciating, or in the least of comprehending them, so as to imitate and realize them by the exercise of a creative wisdom and energy of his own.

But he continues (20th verse): *And will show him greater things than these, that ye may marvel.*

It would seem, then, that the entire field of the divine ideas and works are not presented to the Son even, in a single view, that there is even to him a gradual unfolding of the divine designs and works—that there are things which have not yet been fully disclosed even to him, but have, notwithstanding, been indicated and foreshadowed in such a way that he speaks of them as of things already within his knowledge. In the exercise of his earthly ministry he has healed the sick and performed a variety of other miracles; but there are further developments in store for them, in which he intimates they may see something at which to marvel—as though they had not yet marveled at anything which he had done—had thus far in his works seen nothing worthy of their special wonder. They had, indeed, expressed astonishment at the cure of the man whose case is the occasion of the present discourse. But what was most the matter of their amazement was not the divine goodness and power shown in the cure, but the disregard of the authority and sanctions of the Sabbath. The act of healing, itself, seemed to be looked upon by them as an altogether commonplace affair, hardly worth notice at all, and which would not have been noticed if it had not occurred on the Sabbath. He forewarns them that in the developments of the not distant future, events are in store for them in which they may find something to engage their attention besides the day on which they take place or their bearing on the question of the supremacy and perpetuity of the Jewish polity. He goes on to indicate something in regard to what the nature of those events will be.

The aim and the import of the statements and explanations which he here makes to the Jews in a practical and concrete form, when formally and concisely expressed, is this: that in the scale of universal being, he is equal with the Father as being equally with him within the order of the Godhead, from which as from its infinite and eternal fountain-head all created life and being proceeds, and thus, equally with the Father, holding the supreme rank in the general scale of being; but while, equally with the Father, he has, by right of nature, his place within the Godhead, he is not yet equal with him in it.

This plainly presents a view of the nature of the Trinity not at all in accordance with the orthodox standards; which require that the Son should not only be equally with the Father within the Godhead—but absolutely *equal* with him in it. It is not sufficient that we assert that there are three persons in the Godhead ; orthodoxy requires more. It requires that we hold not only to the three persons, but to their absolute coequality, both of nature and of rank ; for it maintains that they cannot each of them be God without being equal in all respects to each other. But neither is this all that orthodoxy requires. For, if this were all, then it would seem to follow that the Godhead is a thing consisting of three exactly equal parts, and each of the three parts constituting it—each of the three persons must therefore be the third part of God. This, of course, is inadmissible ; for the doctrine is that each of the three persons is the whole of God. It is required, therefore, that we hold, as orthodoxy does hold, that each of the three persons comprehends within himself the entire contents of the Godhead, the inevitable result of which is that in the three persons we have the Godhead *three times over.* In other words, not a trinity of persons in the one Godhead, *but a Trinity of Godheads !*

The Godhead, therefore, cannot be conceived of as a monad—or as an abstract unity—or as absolutely one and simple in its essence, for that would be not to have any essence at all. Neither can it be conceived of as a single person, for that would be the direct denial of any such thing as a Trinity in any sense. Neither can it be conceived of as consisting of three co-equal and coördinate persons, dividing the substance of the Godhead equally among them; nor as three persons, each comprehending in himself the entire substance of the Godhead, for that would be to make three Godheads, which is absurd, and contrary to the supposition, which is that there is but one. It remains as the only possible mode of conception that the Godhead be regarded as constituting *an organic Unity* of being, distinct and supreme over all other being, having at the same time, within it, as the nature of an organic Unity requires, the distinction of greater and less, of organic life and organic principle of life. For there can be no such thing as a unity of life that has not the principle of its life as well as of its unity within itself. It cannot be *united in anything whose existence is outside of itself.*

Thus, all obscurity and all difficulty is removed from the declaration of our Lord, a declaration on which the doctrine of the Trinity is mainly grounded, and out of which it has grown, and without which, and the connected declarations, no such doctrine as that of the Trinity would have been incorporated in the standards of the church. There is, according to the view above given, no difficulty in understanding him when (John x. 30) he says: "I and my Father are One," and (John xiv. 28) "My Father is greater than I;" we see how both these declarations can be true, and how all seeming inconsistency between them is removed. If we regard the Godhead as an organic unity, not as a single person or individual, but as a system of being having personal distinctions within itself, it is plain that when he says that he and his Father are one, he means to assert that his person and that of his Father constitute the unity of the divine nature, that the Godhead is a unity, and that he and his Father are equally elements in it, whilst at the same time he is distinct from him and subordinate to him.

Generally, or generically speaking, the Father and the Son are one, there is no difference of nature between them; but individually and particularly speaking, there is a difference between them; and that not a difference as between individuals of the same rank and of the same species, but a difference of rank, though of the same species,—the Father and the Son not standing in relation to each other as one man to another, nor as coördinate branches from a common root or vine; but they are related to each other as the branch is related to the vine, or the individual and particular members of a species to their common principle or fountain-head.*

* For the judgment and opinions of the early Greek fathers on this subject of the Trinity, and as showing the ideas that were entertained upon the subject in those early times (of comparative purity and piety of life and of doctrine) when men had ideas upon it, and when it was a living and a leading topic, and stood in the fore-front of Christian thought and life and doctrine, see Cudworth's Platonic Christian's Apology,—Intellectual System,—Vol. I., Book IV.—pp. 777–804.

I take this opportunity to add that it would be natural that the ordinary mind should look upon the generation of the Son in the same light as upon the generation of creatures, that is, not as having its ground in the Divine Essence just as the production of branches and fruit has its ground in the nature of the vine ; not conditioned upon any single act of the divine will, but rather preceding all such individual and particular acts. The Arian error lay just here: they could not distinguish between the act of the divine will by which the creature nature is brought forth, and that necessity of the divine Essence, independent of all particular volition, by which the Son is begotten out of the divine Essence, and out of a necessity of the divine nature as subsisting in the Father, the fountain-head of the Godhead, and so one with it, and the very same nature in its developed form. Whence, then, comes the Post-Nicene conception of the co-equality of the persons as necessary to the real and true divinity and Godhead of each? There is certainly no hint of it in any of the discussions, or in the creed finally adopted by the Nicene council, unless it is contained in the term Homoonsion (consubstantial). And that no such idea is contained in that according to the Athanasian sense, or any sense that was put upon the term by the Council, or before it, is certain. What the Athanasian sense was is clearly given, and by that sense and the similitude by which Athanasius illustrated it, that interpretation is excluded and rendered impossible. He compares the unity of Essence in the Father and the Son to the organic unity of life in the vine and its branches : and the difference of rank and power between the Father and the Son in the Godhead, to that between the vine and the branches in one and the same living tree, or vine. According to this, while the Son is one and the same in Essence with the Father, he is no more equal with him than the branch is equal with the vine. Whence, then, came the doctrine of the co-equality of the persons, and the idea that Christ could not be truly God unless he were in all respects the equal of the Father, and standing on an absolutely equal footing with him in the unity of the Godhead? It is evidently a gross corruption of the true doctrine. It must have been "unawares and privily brought in" to supplement the true doctrine as it stands in the creed, and as it was understood and adopted by the Council. The result, if not the covert design, was to put an effectual stop to all discussion of the main topic, and especially to guard more effectually against the possibility of any foothold being ever gained for Arianism within the orthodox definition—to guard against the possibility of any Arian interpretation being put upon it in the future, and thus against the possibility of any future questions or disputes upon the thing intended by the definition. If such was the design, it must be confessed that it has proved a most signal and entire success, so far as the history of the doctrine from that time to this is concerned. (See Neander, Vol. II., p. 391, Note.)

IV.

Titles, personal and substantive, in which Name and Nature are identical:
The Son of Man and the Good Shepherd.

THE titles by which Christ is known in Scripture are numerous, and all of them more or less significant; but the two which he applied to himself, which yet can hardly be said to be applied to him at all by any one else, are of special significance with reference to his nature and the relations which he sustains to humanity. In fact, it is of little use for us to inquire as to what he may be in himself, or in his other relations, if we leave out of the account or do not make prominent the relation which he sustains to us. It is in this relation only that we can understand or have any intelligible idea of him. The same is true respecting God in the general sense of the Godhead. If we know him at all, it must be practically. As a pure abstraction, or an object of purely intellectual apprehension, without reference to our practical and experimental relations to him, he is in reality nothing to us, for the simple reason that he is unknown to us. All ideas of God that are ideas or intellectual conceptions merely, and that do not include knowledge acquired by experience, are powerless in their influence upon us, and have, in fact, no sure foundation of even rational evidence to stand upon. The idea of a merely speculative knowledge of God that does not rest upon and is not derived from experience, is a mere dream. Without experience we are without the data from which alone anything like solid or tenable conclusions can be drawn.

Wherefore, I say, that these titles which Jesus most delighted in, and which he was certain to give to himself when he specially wished to put us in a situation to understand what he was in reference to us, and the nature of the office which he came to discharge in our behalf, are of special importance, and deserve much more of attention and thought than they have ever received. Indeed, they belong to the data which he has himself given, and without which we shall be likely to fail in our attempts to attain to the true knowledge of Christ. In regard to these titles, important as they are and manifest as it is upon the very face of them that they contain fundamental truth, it is very surprising that they should have received so little attention, and been almost entirely overlooked by theologians in the construction of their theories of the nature, the person, and the offices of Christ. They seem to have contented themselves with general and loose views, and even vague conjectures concerning their import. No one seems to have supposed that any important light respecting the greatest of all questions—the relation which Christ sustains to humanity—could be gained from the study of that one striking and altogether unique title which, above all others, he delighted to apply to himself when speaking of himself in his general relations, and especially when he had in view the relation which his nature sustains to ours. The consequence is that these titles have been passed by, or left among matters of minor or merely incidental interest, as having either no distinct and definite meaning at all, or at least none of any consequence with reference to fundamental points of doctrine or to philosophic insight into the nature and relations of the God-man.

The titles to which I refer, are the Son of Man and the Good Shepherd.

The first is of very frequent use in the Gospels, and is used by Jesus himself in speaking of himself, much more frequently than any other. Judging not only from the frequency with which it occurs, but from its being scattered indiscriminately throughout the four Gospels, and as common in one as another of them, being therefore not at all a matter pertaining to the style of the particular writer, or depending on his particular taste or point of view; and being used by Jesus on all occasions and without regard to the particular subject of discourse, it is fair to conclude that it was often, nay, almost always, on his lips, and the designation which under all circumstances he was most apt to use in speaking of himself. Whatever the subject of discourse, and whether addressing himself to Jew or to Gentile, learned or unlearned, friend or foe, this was the name by which he almost invariably called himself; for the simple reason, doubtless, that it seemed most natural to him, and was at all times uppermost in his thoughts. Besides, it was no more than natural that, being so in his, he should wish to make it so in ours.

It is worthy of remark, at the same time, that it was not used in speaking to or of him either by his disciples or the Jews, and that it scarcely occurs, if indeed at all, in the Apostolical Epistles. The truth probably is, that for the most part the term conveyed no definite meaning even to his disciples; and seemed to them to be arbitrarily used, or in a sense too recondite or too vague for them to inquire into, or expect to understand at all. Besides, the term, from being not a proper name, but rather a general term, implying in its form something abstract and general, rather than anything personal or individual in its meaning, was obviously unsuitable as an appellative, or term of personal address, and could not be used as such without violence to the laws of thought and of speech.

In the most general sense the use of the term is based upon the organic conception of the world, and its relations to God; but this conception long ago dropped out of the human mind, or at least out of its conventional methods and its philosophical theories; and our systems of philosophy, of interpretation and theology, have been based upon theories of an altogether different sort, which have only served to cast darkness rather than light upon our pathway, and to lead us astray from the natural interpretation of Scripture as well as of the works of God.

This organic conception of the world, however, was not unknown to the fathers of philosophy--Plato and Aristotle; and if one with the character and claims of Jesus had presented himself to them *as not any particular man, but the Son of Man*, they would have been at no loss to divine his meaning, and would inevitably have understood him as claiming to be divine and not merely human; as having original and creative elements in him, and not merely those which are creaturely.

The perennial freshness which still belongs to the works of these philosophers, is owing almost entirely to this organic mode of conceiving of the universe, which permeates their thinking from beginning to end. Modern thought, tired by its long and fruitless wanderings in the wilderness of shadows and of lawless and lifeless speculation, is turning back more and more to the old masters, and asking for the old paths. It has but to find, and walk and continue in them, in order to find rest to its soul, and fruit and satisfaction as the result of its toils. When that day comes theology will become a new science, and the arbitrary and tyrannical dicta and decrees of councils will no longer be the source of our inspiration; but we shall resort to the same fountains of living water to which such fathers as Origen, Clement, and Athanasius himself resorted. Then, intellect will awake from the death of its centuries of bondage and servility, and theology as well as all other science will make progress; and the Church will be coming rapidly, in the unity of the faith and of the knowledge of the Son of God, unto a perfect regenerate and elect humanity, unto the measure of the stature of the fullness of Christ. The Son of Man will then, for the first time, be enthroned in our philosophies and our theologies, and reign supreme in them as well as in our hearts.

The most that has hitherto been made out by the commentators with reference to the signification of the title is, that it is meant to affirm or imply something in relation to his humanity; exactly what, or whether anything of any particular consequence, they are by no means prepared to say. They think that it was undoubtedly intended to indicate, in a general and loose way, something concerning his relations to the human race. That it is a term by which he sought not so much to instruct us in regard to his nature, as to draw us near to him in love and confidence, and to assure us of the intimacy of the relation which he sustained to us, and the tender regard he felt for us as men.

If it is asked what definite meaning he had, the answer is, of course, he could have meant no more and no less than to say that he was human; or, in other words, that he was, as each of us is, *a man.* Speaking as he does, as to his humanity, he could not mean to say that he was any more or any less than a man, for, according to the assumed theories, he must be *a man* in order to be human at all. He means, then, by the title to tell us that he is human, but that he could be in no other way than by being *a man.* A man, therefore, he was, and that is the end and whole of the matter. This is the sum total of the light which theology has thus far cast upon the question, the upshot of all which is, that the use of the term was a singular, obscure, and enigmatical way of saying that though related to the Father as his only-begotten Son, he was at the same time to be looked upon and treated by us as a fellow-man, in all points tempted like as we are, yet without sin.

Now, this would be conclusive, and here we should be obliged to rest the whole matter, if it were indeed so (as it is not) that there is no way in which he could have humanity and be really and truly human, except by being actually, so far as his humanity is concerned, nothing but *a man*.

The entire mistake, the manifold darkness and confusion, the utter failure on the part of theology thus far to entertain a rational and scriptural idea of the humanity of Christ, has this origin. This false philosophy respecting race and species; this failure to reach and accept the ancient organic conception of the world; this arbitrary and baseless *nominalism*, taking the place of a rational and scriptural *realism*, is the *fons et origo malorum*, " the direful spring " of the evils of our theology, and has made any rational conception either of the Godhead or of the manhood—any just conception of the relation of the one order to the other, an impossibility. It is owing to this that since the Council of Nice, darkness has settled down on the doctrines of the Trinity, and of the nature and person of Christ, and theology (in the strict and proper sense) has groped at noonday, as in the night.*

The truth of philosophy and of Scripture is, that without something more than individual and particular men there could be no such thing as what we mean by the human species. Without something more than the particular and separate members of an order, whether of plants or of animals, there could be no such thing as race or species. Without a common fountain-head out of which they spring, and in which they find the principle of their life and their unity, how do they ever come to exist at all? Creation is not sporadic, it is organic. It is not the repetition of so many separate

---

* It is very surprising and deeply to be lamented, that while Athanasius held to the *consubstantiality* of the Father and the Son in the Godhead, and illustrated it by the similitude of the vine and its branches, he should yet have denied and denounced as savoring of Arian heresy the consubstantiality of Christ and humanity in the order of the Human which the similitude was used by Christ expressly to illustrate. Whilst thus in regard to the first he was a great light, leader and benefactor, in regard to the second he was a great *misleader* and propagator and perpetuator of error, darkness and confusion in theology. It is to us that Christ says, I am the vine, ye are the branches, and not of the Father, he is the vine and I am the branch,—though the illustration applies, and was doubtless intended to apply to both the orders: yet to the first, the Divine order, it is applied indirectly and by implication and analogy; whilst to the latter, the Human order, and the relation of Christ to men, in that order, it applies directly and expressly.

acts, without any organic relation between them —without any such relation as that of original and copy, vine and branches, head and members among them. All life is systematic, not only in its form, but in its origin. It is so in form, because it is so in origin, and according to the law of its creation. The individual in all cases, and in all the orders of which living nature is composed, belongs to a species, and there is no such thing, and there never was any such thing, as an individual existing alone before the existence of its species. Individuals are not first formed, and then species afterwards out of them by comparison and combination, or the "selection of the fittest." But in the order of nature the species is formed first, and the individuals afterwards. There is in all cases a common source and origin in nature to which they are to be referred, and by reference to which their common characteristics or specific likeness is to be explained. The specific principle, idea, or archetype does not exist separately from and subsequently to them (according to the doctrine of nominalism), but in organic union with them, and together with them forming the organic unity of the species, or race of being. Every individual has in him something more than his mere individuality or individual and particular characteristics. A universal element enters into each particular member of a species in virtue of which they constitute a species, and become recognizable and known as members of such or such a race, and receive the common name by which it is distinguished from all other races. There is, therefore, in every individual of a species or member of a race, a *race element*, by which it is distinguished from the members of all other races, and *individual* and *particular* elements by which it is distinguished from all the other individuals of its own race,—thus, in every particular man, there is that which belongs to him as a man, and which determines his race, and that also which distinguishes him from all other men, and by which he is recognized and known as that particular man.

This is the realism of nature, of Scripture, and of the ancient philosophers, as might be abundantly illustrated by reference to their works. And there occurs in Plato a passage wherein he designs distinctly to set forth this doctrine, which, notwithstanding its length, I venture to introduce. It is from the tenth Book of the Republic:

" Well, then, shall we begin as usual by bringing a number of individuals which have a common name under one form or idea?"

"That has been our usual plan. Do you understand me?"

"I do."

"Let us take any instance; there are beds and tables in the world, and many of them. Are there not?"

"Yes."

"But there are only two ideas, or forms, of them; one the idea of a bed, the other the idea of a table."

"True."

"And the maker of either of them makes a table for our use in accordance with the idea—that is our way of speaking of this and similar instances--but he does not make the ideas themselves?"

"Certainly not."

"And there is another artist—I should like to know what you would say of him."

"Who is he?"

"One who is the maker of all the works of all other workmen!"

"What an extraordinary man!"

"Wait a little, and there will be more reason for your saying that. For this is he who makes not only vessels of every kind; but plants and animals, himself and all other things—the earth and heaven, and the things which are in heaven or under the earth; he makes the gods also."

"He must be a rare master of his art."

"Oh! you are unbelieving, are you? Do you

mean that there is no such maker or creator, or that in one sense there might be a maker of all these things but not in another? Do you not see that there is a way in which you could make them yourself?"

"What is this way?"

"An easy way enough; or rather there are many ways in which the feat might be accomplished; none quicker than that of turning a mirror round and round, and catching the sun and the heavens and the earth and *yourself*, and other animals and plants, and all the other creatures of art as well as nature, in the mirror."

"Yes," he said, "but that is an appearance only."

"Very good," I said; "you are coming to the point now; and the painter, as I conceive, is just a creator of this sort—is he not?"

"That is true."

"But then, I suppose, you will say that what he creates is untrue. And yet there is a sense in which the painter also creates a bed."

"Yes," he said, "but not a real bed. And what of the maker of the bed? Were you not saying that he does not make the idea, which, according to our view, is the essence of the bed, but only a particular bed?"

"Yes, I did say that."

"Then, if he does not make that which exists he cannot make true existence, but only some semblance of existence; and if any one were to say that the work of the maker of the bed, or of any other workman has real existence, he could hardly be supposed to be speaking the truth. At any rate," he replied, "philosophers would say that he was not speaking the truth. Can we wonder, then, that there is an indistinctness about his work, too, when compared with truth?"

"No, indeed."

"Suppose that we inquire into the nature of this imitator, as seen in the examples given?"

"If you please."

"Well, then, here are three beds; one is natural [the species] which, as I think that we may say, is made by God. No one else can be the maker."

"No."

"There is another, which is the work of the carpenter?"

"Yes."

"And the work of the painter is a third?"

"Yes."

"Beds, then, are of three kinds, and there are three artists who superintend them; God, the maker of the bed, and the painter."

"Yes; there are three of them."

"God—whether from choice or from necessity—made *one bed*, and *only one;* two or more such ideal beds, neither ever have been or ever will be made by God."

"Why is that?"

"Because, even if he had made but *two*, still a third would appear behind them in which the idea of both of them would be contained, and *that would be* the ideal bed and not the two others."

"Very true," he said.

"God knew this, and he desired to be *the real maker of a real bed*, and not a particular maker of a particular bed, and therefore in nature he created one bed only." [In other words, God does not directly create the individuals of a species; but he is the author of the ideal from out of which they all spring.]

This is the true theory of race and species, and furnishes the means for the settlement of the question respecting the relation which Christ sustains to humanity. It shows the possibility of his belonging to humanity, and being in the most vital and eminent sense human, without being any particular man. He is, according to the illustration of Plato, that species or fountain-head, out of which all particular men spring.

If, in order that there may be such a thing as the

human race it is necessary that there should be something besides the aggregate of individual and particular men, may not Christ be that *something besides?* If, in every man, along with his individual element, there must be also an universal race-element by the possession of which he is constituted human, may not Christ be that universal element—*that in every man in virtue of which he is a man?* This, beyond doubt, furnishes the key to the interpretation of the title the Son of Man. It means *humanity*, not in its individual members, but in its root. He means by it to say to us, *I am the principle of your humanity, or your humanity in its principle—I am the vine, ye are the branches.* What is meant, then, when it is maintained that he is human and yet not *a man*, is that he is the root, and not one of the branches of our humanity.

Of that race of which we ourselves are particular members merely, he is the universal and root element. Of that of which we are only the particular and successive manifestations in time, he is the original and eternal principle and fountain-head, *Jesus Christ, the same yesterday, to-day, and forever.*

No mere nominalism in philosophy can enter into the conception of the unity of the race in Christ. The principle of species is no generalized abstraction, the production of our own minds, and found necessary for the purposes of order and distinctness in our conceptions. It is not an arrangement which we make for our own convenience, for the purposes of classification and system; nor is it a mere subjective necessity imposed upon us by the inherent laws of thought in our own minds. It is no *universalia post rem* (to use the formula of the schools), as the nominalists claim; but *universalia ante rem, et in re*, according to the realism of nature and of true philosophy.* We must regard Christ in his relation to humanity as that universal—that principle of unity which is at the same time the source and principle of life and being. Without Christ, as the universal element in humanity, existing first and before the foundation of the world as its eternal, original, and first principle, the existence of any such thing as the human race is inconceivable and manifestly impossible. It is not merely a creator that is needed, but a creator who enters as the principle of life and of unity into the race which he creates and makes it a species and a living and organic unity. It is not, then, in the sense of any abstraction or mere subjective construction, the necessary fruit and condition of our own thinking, that Christ calls himself the Son of Man, but in a sense the

* See Uberweg's History of Philosophy, Vol. I., p. 366, §§ 91, 92.

most original, the most real—independent of time and of all fruits, or modes, or laws, or necessities of our thinking. It is not a form or a condition of our *thought* merely, but of our very existence. It is not that we cannot think except in that way. and upon that hypothesis, but that it is owing to that that we exist, and that there is any such thing as the human mind or the human race at all.

The article "the" which is inseparable from the title, and an integral part of it, grammatically speaking, makes it impossible to use it as an appellative. We cannot address an individual as *the* Son of man—or as *the* man. If, therefore, the disciples had used the title in addressing him. they would have been obliged to drop the article, and to say: "Son of man" or "man"—a change entirely inadmissible, as being nothing short of a radical perversion, and the use of a liberty for which there was no warrant or excuse in the term as Christ used it. "Son of man" is an address used in the Old Testament, and as there used is personal and appropriate, and means no more than we mean by the term "man" in addressing an individual. But the disciples never addressed their Lord in this way. It would have been a freedom which they had neither any right or disposition to use. It would have been positively disrespectful as used towards one so much their superior, and would have done violence to the feelings of instinctive reverence and awe with which they regarded him. Furthermore, in writing of him, the apostles do not use the title. The only exception is in the Apocalypse, where John sees "One that was like the Son of man." The majesty and glory of his appearance correspond to and recall that indefinable and awful sense of something really human yet above humanity, that was conveyed to the mind of the apostle when in the days of his flesh he was accustomed to hear him speak of himself as the Son of man. Of course this which the apostle adopted in the apocalyptic vision would be a usage unsuitable entirely to sober prose, or ordinary didactic discourse, where we deal with the literal conceptions of the understanding and not with the ecstasies of feeling, or high-wrought creations of the prophetic or poetic imagination. The term the Son of man is didactic, and gives not so much the literal name, as the theory and philosophical significance of the object to which it is applied. This is sufficient to account for the absence of the term from the ordinary apostolic writings. It was not that even after the gift of the Spirit, they did not understand it, but that they chose to convey their ideas of the nature and person of Christ in other language. The use of the phrase in doctrinal discourse, as Christ used it, would have led them into a field of explanation and philosophical analysis and disquisition which it was foreign from their purpose to enter.

But this is no excuse for theologians whose professed object is to do just what it would have been inconsistent with the nature of the apostolic office to have done, viz., to unfold philosophical relations and distinctions, and build up systems of doctrine upon grounds of philosophical reason and necessity. I am not aware, however, that any theologian has attempted to unfold or even ventured so far as to indicate the philosophical principle which may be supposed to underlie this title, the Son of man, frequently as Christ used it, and fond as he evidently was of applying it to himself. It is evident that he, at least, saw something specially and deeply significant in it, and something which strongly endeared and recommended it to him. It is evident that better than any other within the compass of Jewish speech, it answered his own unclouded, uppermost, and most impressive idea of himself, as he stood related to that human nature in the midst of which he tabernacled, and whose flesh he had taken upon him. To our minds there may be something vague in it, and it may fail, unaccustomed as we are to the idioms of the language in which he spake, to convey any clear or distinct meaning, or to make any deep impression upon our hearts. But it was not so with him. He did not use terms which he did not understand; nor of whose fitness he stood in any doubt. Whatever language had to meet his wants, to express his ideas, was at his ready command, and offered itself spontaneously to him as his willing and obedient servitor. He used the term, therefore, because of all the terms which the language of his time and nation afforded, it was the one best fitted to his purpose, and most accurately expressive of the relation in which by nature he stood to mankind, and the one which, when they should come to understand it, would convey to them more light in regard to his essential nature and the mutual relations between him and them than any other. He who knew so well what was in man, knew also quite as well that there was nothing in the term to render it unintelligible to the human mind, when once that mind should have gained the true point of view with reference to it. It is nothing but a false philosophy—the inveterately strong hold which false and mechanical ideas of the relations between God and the universe have taken and do naturally take—that has kept the Christian world so long in darkness on this cardinal point, and made that most profound and significant title the "Son of man," as applied by Christ to himself, so long a root out of a dry ground—an enigma and a stumbling-block to the modern theological mind.

Such, then, is the philosophy of scripture and of nature upon this vital point of Christian doctrine. Such an element as the Son of man must there be in human nature in order that there may be any such thing as human nature in the creation at all. This human that is not particular nor individual, nor created, must there be in humanity in order that there may be any such thing as a race bearing that name and possessing those attributes. And since the race unquestionably exists, and such a thing as that uncreated universal must have existed and must exist as the *conditio sine qua non* of its existence, it follows that such a thing is, and that Christ, who calls himself the Son of Man, is that thing,—that original, eternal source and model of our personal and individual humanity. But whence this term? Do the words on their very face, and in their most obvious sense, convey that idea? They do not. The term "Son" does not by itself and on the face of it, carry the idea of source or origin, or of the universal, the genetic, or the generic. But notice that it is not to be taken by itself, but in its connection in the phrase, as an integral and modifying element of it as a whole. Notice, also, that the term "Man," which follows it, is not preceded by the indefinite article. It is not the Son of *a* Man that he calls himself, as though he were the only son of some particular man, nor *a son of a man*, which is no more than every other man might say of himself, and yet convey no meaning at all, except an empty truism. But if, in the ordinary sense, he were a son at all, he must be the son of some particular man—not of mankind in general. But it is of man in general, and not of any particular man, that he is said to be the Son. But it is impossible that in the sense of a descendant of humanity he should be descended *from mankind in general*, and not from any particular man. He could not get into the race in any such general way as that. There is but one way of getting in, and that is by descent from some particular man who is his natural and actual father. The door into the race is a particular and concrete, and not an abstract and general one. To say that he is a child of the race, yet not of any particular member of it, is simply to talk nonsense. But if he were a descendant in the natural and only possible sense, the article "the" would not be applied to him. He would, like any other man, be *a* son. It is not possible, the laws of language do not permit, it is not within the possibilities of rational speech, to call any man *the son of man.* It is obvious, therefore, that in calling himself such he meant to deny that he was *a man.* He could not more emphatically have denied his human origin than he did by calling himself by this title, unless he meant to set all usage at defiance and use words in utter disregard of any known sense or acceptation. How perfectly preposterous, then, it is, to say that what he meant by the phrase in question to affirm is just that which according to its necessary construction and only possible acceptation, he must have meant to deny. The sense of a human origin or descent from the race by any sort of generation, natural or supernatural, cannot by any possibility be extracted or extorted from the words.

Whence, then, the origin of the phrase, and why is it used to express the sense which we have given it, and which, in the nature of things, it is necessary to give it? I answer, that it is a Hebrew idiom. It is a form of expression used in the Old Testament to express humanity in the generic sense, and means the same as and is equivalent to the term "man" in the general sense. It is, then, a generic term borrowed from the Hebrew, to express "man" or "humanity." But the idea of humanity has two aspects, according to the point of view from which it is regarded. It can be viewed in the light of its generic principle, or in that of its particular manifestations or products,—in the light of its organic spirit and life principle, or of its body, consisting of the organized aggregate of its members,—in the light of its root or of its branches,—in the light of the particular individuals which, taken together, make up its outward species, or of the universal element underlying, entering into, and uniting them all into the unity of a distinct race.

It is in this latter sense—that of the universal and creative principle—that Christ calls himself "humanity." Instead of using the word man in the generic sense, and saying I am *man*—humanity itself, whilst you are only men partaking of humanity, he uses the equivalent, more expanded and softer term, and distinguishes himself from us, and indicates his generic relations by calling himself *the Son of Man.* A marked instance of this use of the phrase in the Old Testament, and one, too, of which particular notice has been taken by St. Paul, and to which a marked theological significance has been assigned by him, is found in the eighth Psalm: "*What is man,*" the Psalmist exclaims, "*that thou art mindful of him,* or *the Son of man,* that thou visitest him?" The Apostle argues (Heb. 2) that these words contain a reference to Christ, and maintains that by the term the Son of man here Christ is meant, and he goes on to prove the point by comparing the different parts of the Psalm with each other, and showing that as a whole the Psalm has its fulfillment in him, and cannot be interpreted without reference to him, nor without understanding the term the *Son of man as meaning him.*

The Psalmist says of the Son of man (5th verse), Thou hast crowned him with glory and honor, (6th), Thou madest him to have dominion over the works of thy hand, thou hast put *all things* under his feet. But (the apostle rejoins) we do not see yet all things put under him. We do not, that is, see the human race occupying a position of supreme dominion over the whole creation; on the contrary, the position of man with reference to the lower creation is to a great extent one of subjection and bondage—he is the slave rather than the master of his circumstances. How, then, he asks, is an explanation of these words in accordance with the facts in the case possible? His answer is, we have the explanation of the words, the removal of the seeming contradiction, if we consider Jesus to have been actually intended, or humanity in the person of Jesus—by the term, man, or the Son of man. For, he says, we do see Jesus, who was made a little lower than the angels for the suffering of death, crowned with glory and honor, that he by the grace of God should taste death for every man. Man considered in his individual capacity, and meaning the aggregate of the individuals of the species, seems to be in a low and servile condition, and wholly unworthy of ranking as the undisputed and glorious sovereign of the universe.

In comparison with the Heavens, the work of the divine fingers, the moon and the stars which God has ordained, he seems the most transitory, trivial, and insignificant of creatures, and wholly unworthy of notice in comparison with the grand displays of the glory of the creation in the heavens above; but not so when he is considered as in the person of the Son of man, whom the Father has appointed heir of all things, by whom also he made the worlds, who being the brightness of his glory and the express image of his person, and upholding all things by the word of his power; when he had by himself purged our sins, sat down on the right hand of the majesty on high, and to whom it is said: And thou, Lord, in the beginning hast laid the foundations of the earth; and the heavens are the works of thine hands. They shall perish, but thou remainest, and they all shall wax old as doth a garment, and as a vesture shalt thou fold them up, and they shall be changed; but thou art the same, and thy years shall not fail.

We have reached the point proposed. The question what is the significance of the title, the Son of man, so absolutely unique, as a personal designation without precedent, without resemblance, almost without analogy in the nomenclature of thought or of things—but yet so manifestly the favorite of our Lord himself, and applied by himself to himself by evident and strong partiality—the question has received its answer. Within the scope of human thought or inquiry, there is no greater one, and the attainment of the point of view from which we are able to give it a clear and satisfactory answer is one of the greatest, certainly one of the most fruitful within the reach of our faculties. For it presents the substance underlying the greatest of all the names by which the Incarnate Deity can be known, the light in which he is brought most nearly home to our practical thoughts and apprehensions, the reality in the light of which he most loved to contemplate himself, and most desired to have us contemplate him.

This, the reaching of the requisite intellectual and moral points of views from which to understand him, he knew could be accomplished only by education—which he also knew would require much thought, time, and experience; the experience which comes only from thought and time, and the thought which can come only as the fruit of time and experience. We must, he knew, have time to escape the fallacies and the frauds of the outward senses—of the sensuous imagination—of the carnal understanding (the faculty judging according to sense), and above all the snares of education and tradition, and of philosophy falsely so called—the snares of an empty, lifeless, plausible nominalism. We must by the power of thought, and as the result of training in the school of experience and of Christ, come at length to the reality which the mind instinctively craves, and short of which it cannot rest—no mere subjective reality, its own creation to supply its own want, and which it imposes upon itself as objectively real, when in fact there is no such reality—no being answering to the title, the Son of man, except in our own thought, no universal element in humanity answering to the universal in our thought. We must, I say, come not to the subjective universal merely, but to that which is the objectively real—which answers to the necessary form of thought, and this is found only in him who calls himself the Son of man.

May we not say that here the goal of thought is reached, the point beyond which it cannot go—and arrived at which it has no need to go any further? What is the uttermost limit to which thought can attain? the most advanced, the most fundamental and universal position possible for the thought to occupy? I answer, when it becomes not indeed identical with its object, but its actual well-defined counterpart. Say not that where such mental shadow exists there is no corresponding outward reality! but that the shadow is all, and the corresponding outward merely a projection of the inward, the result of the imaginative faculty. Account if you can for the shadow without an object to cast it. Just so certain as the reality of the shadow, so certain is the existence somewhere objectively of the substance that casts it. Though it be but a shadow, it just as much needs to be accounted for as though it were a substance, and can no more exist without a corresponding substance than substance that casts no shadow. It is enough that the thought reflects the object, and that it is the exact image of its original.

In this conception of Christ, as the principle of our humanity, the universal in that organic unity of which we are the particular members (the particular involving the universal as that without which it has itself no significance, no function, no place, and *no existence*), in this conception of Christ as the Son of man, we have the organic conception of humanity, we have the key to the solution of all the problems, not of redemption merely, but of history and philosophy also. In the attributes of that fundamental organic idea, we have reflected all the attributes and all the functions of the God-man, mediator, and medium between the Godhead and man.

Does the church of the living God, out of the profoundest and most universal instincts of her faith and her love, out of the inmost necessity of her own thought, feeling, and experience, hold him to be divine! Does she find her God, her head and her life in him, and worship him as her only Lord, and does she find it impossible to be true to herself and not do it?

Is it impossible for her not to make him head over all things and fountain-head of life and peace to her, and do we not, in this view of the relation in which Christ stands to humanity, find the ground upon which that inherent faith and necessity of hers rest? Is he not, as the principle of our humanity, necessarily divine? Can he be that and not be God? Can humanity have its eternal source and fountain-head —its substance and its principle—in that which is itself merely human or creaturely, and in no respect transcending the creature nature? If we understand ourselves, we mean and can mean by the term "our God" not anything outside of or other than our humanity, nothing that does not in some way come within the sphere of our nature, our actual and immediate knowledge and experience. Nothing that does not come within the sphere of our nature—nothing between us and which there is no communion of nature, and which has nothing in common with us in respect to nature, can be the possible object or matter of our experience. If "our God" comes within the limits of our experience and can be known to us only by experience (and there is no other way in which we can know him), then of necessity his nature in some way comes within the sphere of ours, and there is a community of nature between him and us. At least there is necessarily something in common between his nature and ours implied in the fact that we know and love him, and that he is to us naturally and truly our God.

To this conclusion let us hold fast, as to the sheet-anchor of our hope and the lode-star of our faith in theology as well as in philosophy. It is a conclusion from which there is no escape, except into doubt, prescription, nominalism, mechanism, materialism and intellectual death. It is so that we stand related to God and him to us, or else God is really and virtually no God to us (or which is the same thing in effect), a God of whom we know and can know nothing. The one point necessary to guard, and where the only danger lies, is that the proper distinction be observed and the identity not carried too far. As earnestly as we affirm that he has a nature in common with ours, so earnestly do we deny that he is *a man. He is not one of us, and yet he is all of us and all there is of us, except our imperfections and our sins.* He is the principle of the humanity of every one of us, that in every one in virtue of the possession of which we are men; without him, as the universal in our nature, not one of us, though in the human form, would be a man. Nothing is more certain than this: that if we as men, as a race, had not by nature something in common with each other, we could not love, enter into sympathy with, or even know each other internally at all. *If we had not all of us one human heart*, we should all be strangers to each other, and as destitute of interest in or sympathy with each other, as we are with the beasts that perish, or they with us.

Imagine the chasm, as to all that endears us to each other and ennobles us in our own sight and that of our fellows, that exists between our minds, our experience, our consciousness as men, and that of the brutes: try to conceive the chasm which difference of nature makes in these respects, and you have the chasm which would yawn between God and us, the impossibility there would be of our knowing and loving him and making him our God as we do, if there were nothing in common between his nature and ours.

Here is the point where the second title, *I am the Good Shepherd*, comes first into view. The first of these titles furnishes the key to the explanation of the other. The second limits the application of the first, and reduces it to a concrete and practical form. The second, as the minor term carries the first as its major in its bosom, comprehends it under its more limited and special significance.

I am the Good Shepherd and know my sheep, and am known of mine; *even as the Father knoweth me*, and I *know the Father*, even so do I know *my sheep, and they* me, John x. 14, 15.

The same relations of knowledge and affection,—of knowledge implying affection and affection implying knowledge, as those which exist between the Father and the Son in the Godhead, exist between Christ and his people in the manhood. And the great question is, as to what is implied in this common and mutual understanding and affection which subsists alike between the Father and the Son on the one hand, and between Christ and his people—the good shepherd and his sheep—on the other.

We cannot too strongly emphasize the second clause in the verse containing the title, or the title which he gives to us as counterpart to that which he gives to himself—I am the good shepherd, and know my *sheep*, and am known of mine. With reference to them he calls himself shepherd, with reference to himself, he calls them sheep. The titles are not absolute, they are correlative, and indicate office function and mutual relationship and interdependence, with reference to each other. In defining himself he defines us in our relation to him. He defines himself with reference to what as the Son of man he is to us, and with reference to what none but the Son of man could by any possibility be to us, and he defines us with reference to what as men we must be and could be to no other than the Son of man. Notice the vast elevation at which he places himself above us and the immeasurable difference which he makes between himself and us. Notice the relation which as men, he makes us sustain to him. It is as to two points forcibly illustrated by the relation which the literal shepherd sustains to his sheep. These two points are, 1st, elevation in power, office and function above us, implying, of course, a corresponding inferiority and dependence on our part with reference to him. The 2d is correspondence and sympathy, mutual knowledge, attachment and affection between the parties, making him absolutely necessary to us, and us absolutely necessary to him. In the literal and earthly relation the shepherd is as really dependent on his sheep as they on him, though not in all respects. He gets his livelihood from them, but he is not dependent on them for his life. They did not make him, neither, indeed, did he make them any more than they him. He is no more their creator than they his. In that respect they are quite independent of each other. Their natures are not the same, neither have they, so far as the higher nature of the shepherd is concerned, anything in common. And this is the grand respect in which the comparison does not hold and the illustration is not to the point. The correspondence of the two natures is, however, so great, as to serve as an apt and vivid illustration of the relation between Christ and us; if not as to nature, yet as to function at least. In the literal case, the correspondence between the parties concerned is that of correlates, and is as perfect as though the natures were not in reality two different ones, but only counterparts of one and the same. But Christ and his people are real counterparts, the nature in both is one and the same, as he takes pains to prove to us by the comparison and analogy which at once, and without proceeding a step further, or allowing any other matter to intervene, he adduces. To prevent all possible misunderstanding, to show that, by the comparison of the relation between him and us to that between the shepherd and his sheep, he means not merely resemblance and correspondence between different natures, but counterparts of one and the same nature, he immediately adds, by way of explanation, *Even as the Father knoweth me and I know the Father.* In the light of this explanation, so plain that it cannot be mistaken, we must either admit the community of nature between him and us, or deny that between him and his Father. But the latter we cannot do. We know that he means to affirm as beyond the possibility of doubt or question, as a first truth, *that he and his Father are one*—not two natures, but counterpart elements of the one undivided and indivisible nature of the Godhead. There is no difference of natures in the Godhead, though there is difference of rank between the elements that constitute it. The same exactly holds true in reference to the manhood which Christ and his people together constitute; in that Christ is to us, so far as nature and rank are concerned, exactly what his Father is to him in the Godhead. Thus the Son of man, who is our humanity in its principle and fountain-head—the very essence and substance of our nature, declares himself to be also *the Good Shepherd* to us. In that title, the Son of man, lies the fundamental and universal element and ground of another title—that of the good shepherd.

The latter title containing the former, what of good or of sweetness or joy for men is there that it does not contain? Well may the adjective which we translate *good*, mean also the fair and the lovely; for, if there is anything sweet for the eye of humanity to look upon, it is its own nature in the person of its divine Shepherd. What does he mean, by saying that he is our humanity in its first principle and eternal substance, but that he is the principle, the source and substance of all that is truly good and justly dear and sweet to our humanity? Can there be any good to us that is not comprehended within that? Can he be that to us, and not be to us the synonym of all that is beautiful and good to our nature? Reflect upon it: that which comes home to us and enters into us and feeds and nourishes our faculties and satisfies and gladdens our hearts and truly blesses our souls, can come from no foreign source: it must come from within. Not from our own souls—(it is a great mistake to think that our own souls can themselves be any fountain of good to us,) but from that which is more interior to us than our own souls—from that Eternal substance and fountain-head of our humanity, out of which the soul and all that is truly human, beautiful and good, in it, springs. Must not the particular nature and office of the Good Shepherd, inasmuch as it includes within it and contains wrapped up in its meaning, the whole substance of the universal designation, be the Epitome of all conceivable enduring and sincere good to the nature—to the mind and the heart of man—to human nature in all respects and all possible conditions. Christ, as the Good Shepherd, is in precisely the condition to be all this to man, whilst nothing else can be any part of it to us. The vine sustains to the branch precisely the relation, and is to the branch exactly that which enables it to impart to it everything that, as a branch, it can need, or receive, or that can be good for it, whilst nothing else is in any condition to do it any essential good. Whatever pertains to its life, growth, and fruitfulness comes not from within itself, but from the vine which is its own substance and the fountain-head of its life and well-being and beauty and goodliness. For all that is needful and good for it, it is shut up to its vine, but in being thus shut up to that, it has opened out to it in that all that its nature can possibly need or crave or receive of genuine good. Is there not in a practical and intelligible form, nay, in the form of actual every-day experience, comprehended in this latter title the discharge of every function, the opening out of every fountain, the running out of every stream of supply, of benefit and of blessing, that men can need or desire or conceive? In the nature of the case, no one but he who is himself the life-principle of man's humanity, can discharge the functions of the Good Shepherd to him.

How plain it is, that in the Son of man administering the office and discharging the function of Shepherd everything is comprehended, and that nothing of all that man needs for time or eternity, for life or immortality, for wisdom, righteousness, sanctification or redemption, can come from any other quarter.

THE GOOD SHEPHERD.

Immortality.

To specify in a single point (but a most comprehensive one, surely;) I mean that of our immortality,—rightly considered, all our good is comprehended in that. For without that we are nothing, and nothing is not anything, or of any consequence to us. If we are not naturally immortal—and we shall assume that we are not—whence but from him is our immortality to come? To whom but him are we to look for the gift of it? If the principle of our humanity, that in which it lives and moves and has its being, is not immortal, then surely, we are not, and there is no possibility of our ever becoming so. But if he in his own nature is immortal, and the very principle of immortality—if he who is the very life-principle of our humanity is immortal, then, surely, *we*—if we are in him—are such. If the fountain-head is immortal, the members must be; if the vine is immortal, then such must its branches be. If the Good Shepherd is not merely immortal, but immortality itself in its principle, and if the office which he has undertaken to administer towards us is that of giving us eternal life; that is, of administering himself to us, then surely we cannot fail of receiving the boon unless there shall be some failure in the administration; and on that point he has taken particular pains to assure us. To set the matter of possible failure on his part to do all that he has undertaken forever at rest, and to remove all anxiety and every shadow of a doubt or a fear on that point, he uses very strong language, and in using it he doubtless has this fear that may arise in our minds distinctly in view. "My sheep hear my voice, and I know them, and they follow me, *and I give unto them eternal life*, and they shall never perish; neither shall any man pluck them out of my hand. My Father who gave them me, is greater than all, and no man is able to pluck them out of my Father's hand." As though there might arise a doubt of his power to make good the gift which he has bestowed, and perfectly administer the trust which he had received, he pledges the power of his Father. He lets us here, not only into his own deep and awful earnestness in reference to the execution of the trust which has been committed to him, and his own deep feeling on the subject of the duty he has undertaken to discharge, but also into the manner in which, all-powerful as he is, he falls back upon the power of his Father as being in reality the support, the basis, the source of his own. His own heart does not feel the fullness of triumphant assurance in respect to the eternal issue of his administration until he has fortified himself by referring the whole question back to his Father, and by reminding himself that he and his Father are identified in interest in regard to the grand undertaking, and that his power is engaged to carry it out. This most emphatic allusion to the power of him who is the fountain-head of all power, even in the godhead itself, implies not only the existence of doubts and fears on our part, but the consciousness also, on his, of the existence of evil forces, and those nor far off, nor without consequence, which would, if they could, prevent the carrying out of the great undertaking and thwart the purposes of infinite love, and deprive the sheep of their Shepherd, and the Shepherd of his sheep.

It is plain that to his view there exists a hostile element that has already arrayed itself against his administration, and that will prevent its success if it can. And that hostile element stood there confronting him at that very moment. He saw and felt it, in those proud, scornful, and malignant Pharisees who surrounded him, and were impudently and hypocritically clamoring for clearer and more satisfactory light, as if they wanted to believe but could not, for want of the light which they pretended that he might afford them if he would, but which he unfairly and unjustly withholds from them. He has already given them to understand that he knows them, and penetrates their evil designs—by saying to them: "Ye believe not, because ye are not of my sheep. My sheep hear my voice, and I know them, and they follow me—you follow me not; not for the want of clear and convincing evidence, but because ye are not of the right temper and spirit—but of the evil and wrong—not of the sincere, earnest, and confiding, but of the suspicious, the jealous, the hostile, and malignant." I call particular attention to this feature in our Lord's address, for the sake of suggesting that there reveals itself here an element of *wrath and of judgment in the function of the Good Shepherd*—of wrath that can smite, and burn, and consume, as well as of love that can only warm, and cherish, and bless. He suggests that his office will not be found one of gentleness, meekness, and tenderness towards his enemies; that it will not be found to be to them what it is to his sheep—but that, as it is full of love and tenderness to protect, to defend, and shelter them, so will it be an office of terror and destruction to his enemies, and to whatsoever opposeth and exalteth itself against God in this great work of the Good Shepherd which he is carrying on in the world for the eternal salvation of his elect, and for the sake of which the foundations of the world were laid. And here let me say that the punishments of the divine government are remedial, and *that God does not punish for the sake of punishing.* In other words, that his punishments are not punishments so much as chastisements. When, in the case of a sinner, there is no longer any hope of his repentance or his reformation; when he has become reprobate, he is no longer a proper subject of punishment or of discipline. For the object of the Divine government in its treatment of offenders *is their profit—that they may become partakers of its holiness.* When it is no longer possible that any good to them can come out of the chastisement, it ceases to be administered. The ministration is thenceforth one of wrath, which will be inflicted on the sinner, not for the purposes of vengeance, but of destruction; to put him forever out of the way, so that he can no longer be the source of evil and mischief to the universe. The result and the end of the Divine treatment of the enemies of redemption is either to destroy them or convert them into friends. If the latter cannot be accomplished, they will not be suffered to live to be the sources of misery and mischief; neither will they be preserved in being, in order that they may be punished for their crimes and divine justice have satisfaction in the torments which they suffer. Divine justice reaps no satisfaction from the sufferings of the wicked except in the good that results to them from them. It takes no satisfaction in the infliction of suffering, as such, without reference to any good resulting to the sufferer from it. When his sufferings work out for him the peaceable fruits of righteousness, then it is pleased and satisfied, for then its end is gained. But it takes no pleasure in inflicting sufferings that can result in no good, and that have not for their object the good of the offender and the good of the universe through his good. Nay, so far from its finding any satisfaction or pleasure in such sufferings, it is contrary to its nature to inflict them. It is a false idea of the nature of the attribute to suppose it capable of any such thing, or of taking any delight in suffering that has not for its object, and is not calculated to result in, the good of the sinner. Hence, when all possible remedial treatment has failed of its object, and all hope of the reformation of the evil-doer is gone, it does not suffer him to live that he may go on doing evil, nor does it preserve him in being, in order that it may balance the account by the infliction upon him of everlasting suffering; but the operation of its inherent nature, as expressed and incorporated in the eternal and unchangeable order and nature of things, is such as to destroy him forever from the face of the world on which he is nothing but a foul blot, and in which there is no possibility of his reaching any good to himself, or being anything but a source of grief, and pain, and injury to others.*

This view will serve to give a more rounded and adequate expression to the function of the Good Shepherd. It will show that he has of necessity a twofold function. The full discharge of his function

* The next movement in moral materialism is to establish a scale of equivalents between perverse moral choice and physical suffering. Pain often cures *ignorance,* as we know, as when a child learns not to handle fire by burning its fingers, but it does not change the moral nature. Children may be whipped into obedience, but not into virtue, and it is not pretended that the penal colony of heaven has sent back a single reformed criminal. We hang men for our convenience or safety; sometimes shoot them for revenge. Thus, we come to associate the infliction of suffering with offenses as their satisfactory settlement—a kind of neutralization of them, as of an acid with an alkali, *so that we feel as if a jarring moral universe would be all right, if only suffering enough were added to it.* This scheme of chemical equivalents seems to me, I confess, a worse materialism than making protoplasm Master of Arts and Doctor of Divinity.—Dr. O. W. Holmes, "Mechanism in Thought and in Morals," p. 88.

of love to his sheep, and to all who by any possible means may become his sheep, implies a function of consuming and annihilating wrath to all that are not his sheep and can never by any means be made such or anything but malignant and incorrigible enemies to him and to them.

Such, comprehensively and concisely stated, is Christ to us in his office and function as the Good Shepherd. And certainly if the office involves all this, and all that is implied in this towards us, it must possess the most exalted interest for us, and be regarded by us with emotions of love and gratitude, wonder and praise, such as can be awakened by no other object that can possibly come within the sphere of our rational thought or apprehension. Consider how impressive the view of our dependence upon him when looked at in the light of this shepherd function, which in reference to our immortality he discharges towards us. The sheep gets its support and all that belongs to the preservation, security, and welfare of its life from the shepherd. Though he is not the author of its life, yet such are its wants, such its situation, such its exposures and dangers, that without him it could scarcely survive a single day, so great is the dependence of the sheep upon the shepherd. But ours upon Christ is all this, and a great deal more. To him we owe the life itself, in its principle, as well as all that belongs to its preservation, safety, and well being. That which it is his office to preserve, it belongs also to his office to give. That of which he is, as the Good Shepherd, the preserver and benefactor, he is also, in virtue of the same office, the giver. Suppose now that we have a realizing sense of all this which he is to us, and of all the good to our humanity which is involved in the discharge of these shepherd functions towards us, is it any wonder that in the vision of his face and in the sound of his voice, there should be an ineffable and infinite charm? Would it be any wonder if he should be to us the chief among ten thousand, the one altogether lovely?

In order that among the *many—the members*—there may be any of the true beauty of humanity, there must be in them "the one" who is in himself altogether lovely—imparting of his loveliness to them. The complete beauty of our humanity to our eyes, is in "the one;" its partial derivative beauty may be seen in individual men among its members—who belong to the number and rank of the many that constitute its body. It is the beauty of "the one" absolutely beautiful reflected in the minds, persons, characters and tempers of individual men, that makes them dear and beautiful to us as men.

But as yet this second title, the Good Shepherd, has received only a general consideration at our hands. It has had no logical or grammatical definition. The form of words by which it is expressed has not been considered. But it is worthy of regard in this respect, and requires it in order that the meaning which it contains may be fairly unfolded to us. Like every other formula of human speech, it is made up of words and their collocations and relations. It is a phrase grammatically constructed, and as such requires and admits of grammatical analysis and explanation. The title as constructed, consists of two elements—the *good*, and *shepherd*. Plainly the first as taken by itself is absolute in its signification. It excludes the idea of any particular good thing of its kind, and carries the idea that kind does not really belong to it—or if so, that it is alone in its kind. Thus we may read, and in fact we find, as the matter is analyzed, that we *must* read the words as conveying the sense of *the Good as shepherd.* By "the Good," let us suppose that the absolute is meant—in other words, that God as the absolute and eternal good, is meant by the expression. Thus let us suppose that he, the Good, should actually become and take upon him the office and functions of a shepherd. And then let the question be put, what sort of a shepherd would he be? Could we answer that he would be a *good shepherd?* Certainly not, for that would be to give to him, the absolute and universal, a limited and relative character, and rank him only as *co-ordinate*, one among many others holding the same rank, and of the same kind, which would be to deprive him altogether of the character which we have supposed to belong to him, and thus make the answer false to the supposition upon which the question is founded.

What, then, if we remain true to this supposition, is the only answer which could be given to the question, what sort of a shepherd would "the Good," if he should become shepherd, be? It must preclude all comparison between him and any other—for the absolute cannot be compared. The only possible answer, then, would be: He would be *the good shepherd*, or the Good [*as*] shepherd. There is no escape from this sense of the phrase, without a degradation not only of "the Good," but also of Christ, and understanding him by the phrase as intending merely to distinguish himself in character from bad shepherds, or hirelings, whose own the sheep are not; or to rank himself among the good shepherds as one of them, making him thus merely *a good shepherd* instead of a bad, or merely an individual of the class of good ones. But this utterly fails to represent the idea that Christ had in his mind; not only so, it grossly misrepresents it, and conveys a sense entirely different from any that the language will bear or that Christ intended in giving himself the designation.

This, then, we have in Christ: "the Good"—the one who is God to us, and who alone can be known and loved by us as our God—he, the eternal life-principle, source and substance of our humanity: the Son of man coming down from the unknown height of his elevation above us, and drawing near to us from that unknown and dim distance to which our minds remove him from us when he is merely the object of speculative thought, and when experience and consciousness are not the sources whence we derive our knowledge of him—coming thus down and near to us by revealing himself in our hearts—taking to this end the very form of that humanity of which he is the eternal principle—speaking to us with man's voice, in the very tones, and accents, and sentiments, and feeling of that humanity of which we are conscious within us. In this form, he comes and assumes towards us the office of shepherd to guide us in our darkness, to be our strength in weakness, our consolation in distress, our protection and defense in the midst of danger, and over all the power of evil. More than all, nay, all in one, to be life and immortality, with its blessings and benefits, and with all the guards and guarantees which the eternal love and power of the Godhead can throw around them. Beyond and above all other conceptions, then, of kindness, of condescension, and of benefaction, this must rise in our minds. Must he not in this office be dear to us, the one altogether lovely, and comprehend in that single office all that our minds can conceive of as beautiful and good to our nature? For what is the good—the good in itself and absolutely—that which in itself is the sum and substance of all good to us, but the Son of man? And what to us is the Son of man but the synonym of all that is good—of all the good there is for us as men, whether in time or eternity, in the body or out of the body?

Our humanity, be it observed, taken in the sense of the Son of man, does not exclude God. Nay, it not only includes him, but is He. We have him in it, and nowhere else than in it have we him whom with heart and understanding and appreciation we can call our God—in our humanity, I say, as represented in the nature and person of our Lord Jesus Christ. Surely, then, when as such he assumes the office and function of shepherd to us he must be the good shepherd, such a shepherd as none but the Good himself taking that place and performing that function can be. We can never in its fullness of meaning have the good shepherd until we have the Good himself [as] Shepherd and Bishop of our souls.

It is a great thing, and always matter of the sincerest joy and congratulation among men when a good man, as king, sovereign, or chief magistrate is clothed with the office of shepherd of the people. The gladness with which they hear his voice and follow in his footsteps belongs to the region of the profoundest, and most beautiful, and powerful of our sentiments. There is a something of the unspeakable, the involuntary, the perennial about it. It is a sentiment that never dies out; and though, perhaps, inexplicable and even contrary to our theories, conventions, prejudices, and traditions, and even worldly interests, it is nevertheless irresistible, and we follow it almost whether we will or no, as the sheep follow their shepherd when they hear his voice, and he knows them and calls them all by their names. But what shall we say when it is no longer a good man, one of themselves, tempted in all points like as they are, with their imperfections and *their sins* of selfishness and narrowness, and passion and prejudice to warp and bias him—when, I say, it is no longer a good man, but the Good itself—the principle of all goodness and all manhood in humanity, taking upon himself the shepherd's charge, and ruling over men in the interests of humanity and of goodness, and of these alone?

When this guide and guardian appears and places himself at our head, and undertakes to lead us on our dark and perilous way through the undiscovered deeps of the eternities and the possibilities that lie before us; when this vision dawns on our souls and this light appears, our joy and satisfaction are deep, sincere, unutterable. We seem to hear a voice saying unto us, I am the light of the world. He that followeth me shall not walk in darkness, but shall have him who is himself the life—shall have him who is the very fountain-head of the life of his humanity, for his light and his example! (John viii. 12.) He shall have not merely a maxim, or a code, or a dogmatic system to walk by, but a *life*, and that the life, not of an imperfect, fallible man, himself unable to walk except as some one guides him, but of him who is himself the life of all the true life, goodness, or humanity there is in men. The significance of this fact is greater than our thoughts can fully compass.

But this we may know of it, that then we have realized what the apostle meant by his prayer, when he prayed that Christ might dwell in our hearts by faith—that we being rooted and grounded in love might be able to comprehend with all saints what is the breadth and length and depth and height, and to know the love of Christ which passeth knowledge, that we might be filled with all the fullness of God. When the Good—which to us can be no other than the Godman—comes to execute the office of Chief Shepherd towards us, we are assured on the highest grounds of an absolutely perfect guardianship for man. Consider some of the elements that are involved in it: in the first place, it is God himself in a light and in a nature in which we can know and love —enter into sympathy with him and know that in the innermost depths and tenderest fibres of his own being, he is in perfect sympathy with all that is really human (however imperfect, or however darkened and defiled it may be) in us. It is not one nature striving to know and take an interest in and love another, but the same nature, with a sympathy for all that is even hopeful and not reprobate in us, that is quick, generous, tender, appreciative and forgiving, and which will surely forgive to the uttermost, because he so loves our humanity and is so eager and determined to save it, and so longs that it may not perish, but have eternal life. It is not another nature which, strive as we may, must as to its innermost heart and feeling, be foreign and unknown to us, and a thing with which we can enter into no congenial sympathy and fellowship. There must be a community of nature in the case, or that cannot be which the apostle says is matter of fact between God and us. That which we have seen and heard declare we unto you, that ye also may have fellowship with us: and *truly our fellowship is with the Father and with his Son Jesus Christ.* (1 John i. 3.) Thus we have for the first time the idea of our God, and of our being the objects of his almighty and sympathetic love and care realized to us, when we are assured by the unfailing instinct of our humanity that he is present with us in our nature and in our hearts and in that nature and in those hearts by a mysterious yet real indwelling, exercising towards us the office of supreme guardian, guide and comforter of our souls. But consider another point, which with equal certainty and clearness is involved. What absolute security for *perfect purity and disinterestedness in the administration of his office*—see the impossibility of any personal or selfish interest or consideration entering in and interfering to prevent perfect disinterestedness in the administration of the trust which has been committed to him. Talk you of self, or the bias or makeweight of self-interest or ambition interfering in the case to prevent the concentration of the whole power of the office, and all the ardor of the love to men which it involves within its idea and design, from being directed to the one end and consideration of the welfare of the sheep? Is there any danger or even possibility that in the administration there will be a thought directed to something else besides their good? For who are these that he calls his sheep, and over whom he has assumed this guardianship, possession and care? Are they not men, and can he who is *humanity* have any interest that is adverse to or not accordant, and even identical with, that of men? What is humanity but the love of men? and in loving and in serving them, whom but itself does it love and serve? In serving them does it not in the most effectual, nay, in the only possible way, serve *itself?* What self has humanity, or what self-interest, what object to fasten its affections, its ambitions, or even its covetousness, or its pride upon, except what it finds in man? It has no self anywhere but what it finds and feels in them. It has no self in its own breast which can come in competition for its love, its thought or its care, with that which it finds in the nature and the persons of men. They are its other and counterpart self—the self without—which is the reflex and the projection of the self within. And in this I am not straining a word, or playing with an ingenious abstraction, for the sake of making a point. I am only striving to say what the apostle has already and much better said for me. He throws the whole matter into the most living and concrete form. He illustrates the relation between the Good Shepherd and his sheep, by the symbol of the marriage relation. For Christ is the head of the church, even as the husband is the head of the wife, and the interest he takes in the church is the perfection and the divine original of that which the husband takes in his wife. *So ought men to love their wives as their own bodies.* (Eph. v. 23–32.) For this they must do in order to love them as well as Christ loves his church. They ought to copy the divine original of marriage and abolish entirely any such thing as a love or an interest that can stand between them and the love and the devotion which they feel to their wives. He that loveth his wife loveth himself. For no man ever yet hated his own flesh, but nourisheth and cherisheth it even as the Lord the church, for we are members of his body, of his flesh and his bones. Thus in the love of the husband to his wife we have an example of that which is the only *true* and unselfish self-love which it is possible for a man to exercise. But Christ is the true husband of the church, and the love he feels towards her is the divine ideal of the love of the true husband to his wife; only imperfectly realized, only faintly reflected in the case of a merely human married love, when that is at its height and exists in its greatest perfection. According to this standard, the ideal as we have it in the love of Christ for his church, the only self-love which the husband as such knows anything about, is the love which he bears to his wife. If he regards himself, is solicitous for what concerns his own interest, honor and happiness, that solicitude will be shown by the ardor and personal self-forgetfulness with which he lays himself out to promote her happiness, and devotes himself to her protection and to the promotion of her welfare and interest, so that she may feel that she has the best possible guaranties and securities for all that is dear to her as a wife and a woman in his love.

I think the case is made out. If the Good Shepherd is no other than our humanity itself, then the only self-love possible for him is the love which he feels towards men, the only *self-interest* he can have to influence him is the interest which he feels in them.

Moreover, the apostle, in this illustration, distinctly and fully indorses our interpretation of the title—the Good Shepherd—which is that " the good " which appears in Christ exercising the office of shepherd towards men is no other than our humanity itself in its principle ; that is, in its God. For he says that in loving the church, he loves only what is in reality himself; that his love to her is true, and yet entirely unselfish self-love; that in loving her as he does he exercises the only self-love of which he is capable. For he has no self of his own which is a different thing in nature from the self which he recognizes in them, and to whose interest he devotes himself, and which he embraces, and loves, and cherishes in his church. Here is plainly recognized again the great, universal, underlying principle of the organic unity of Christ and his church—of the Good Shepherd and his flock. For, in loving his sheep he could not love himself and find the best and dearest realization of himself and of his true self-interest in them unless between him and them there was a community of nature, and he and they together constituted but one and the same humanity. There could be no community of self-hood and self-interest between them if they were not organically one, and did not together constitute, not two natures, but only a single nature; that is, a dyad, consisting of two elements—the shepherd and the sheep—the head and the members of that unity, the flock. And thus also, he declares—not impliedly, as in the saying, I know my sheep and am known of mine, even as the Father knoweth me and I know the Father—but he goes on in the next verse to say, furthermore, And other sheep I have which are not of this fold; them also I must bring, and they shall hear my voice, and there shall be *one fold, one shepherd.* (John x. 16.)

Not one fold *and* one shepherd. The supplying the conjunction destroys instead of filling out and more fully expressing the sense. The omission of the connective is intentional and significant. The two elements, in the absence of the connecting particle, constitute and express an organic unity, whereas with the particle they represent the fold and the shepherd as two not only distinct, but separate things, with no organic unity between them. As the clause stands, and as it was intended to stand, it represents the shepherd and his flock as constituting not two single and separate things, but a Dyad, or an organic unity consisting of two correlative elements or forces. *One fold—one shepherd*—fold and shepherd, not two, but one. He carries the idea here that whilst he is really distinct from the fold he is not organically separated from it, but as in nature, one with it, and it one with him.

In saying one fold, and emphasizing the one, he points to the unity of the flock. In adding *one* shepherd, he points to that which is the unitizing principle, or to himself as the principle in and through which the unity of the flock is accomplished. For there can be no such thing as a concrete and living unity where there is no principle of unity. And furthermore the principle of such a unity cannot be a thing outside of and separate from it. It must be in the members united by it, or they cannot become a unity in and by means of it. There can be no doubt that Christ means to represent himself as the principle of the unity of his flock. He would and could not speak of them as being one and constituting a unity in any way but in him. Such being the relation which he sustains to them, the foundation is laid in nature for the administration of the shepherd-office toward them in a manner involving the perfection of all that can enter into the idea of the discharge of sacred official duty.

Of necessity, the office of shepherd of humanity must be exercised by humanity in its principle toward humanity *in its members*, in an absolutely perfect manner. We have in the nature and character of the shepherd the pledge, and the sure guaranty, of an absolutely perfect discharge of all the functions involved, and of all the duty enjoined.

Moreover, Christ as the Son of man—the Good [as the] shepherd and bishop of our souls, addresses himself to that which is universal in our humanity. In virtue of the *universality* of his nature and sympathies, he is capable of doing this; but no other—none who does not comprehend within himself that which is universal in the nature of man is capable of it. But in order that we may be numbered among his sheep that hear his voice and follow him, and to whom he gives eternal life, and who are secured by all the love and all the power of the eternal Godhead from ever perishing, or being by any power in earth or hell plucked out of his hand—this universal element lying at the basis of our humanity, and constituting its very life and spirit, must be developed at least in a degree within us, and become potential in determining our conduct and our feelings towards the Good Shepherd when we shall hear his voice calling after us.

It would almost seem as though it were the one thing needful for a man, in order that he may be truly a man, that he should escape from the narrowness of his education and his prejudices—throw off the trammels of creed and nation, and get breadth of ideas, views, feelings, and sympathies. He must be in a situation to sympathize with whatever is truly human in his fellow-men, and so be brought into a genial and generous friendship with them on the broad ground of their common humanity, before he can be said to be himself truly a man, or the possible subject of the benefits of the office of the universal shepherd of humanity. It would seem that the selfish narrownesses, preferences, and prejudices which belong so naturally, and cling so tenaciously and obstinately to him, without which and without being more or less perverted, blended and corrupted, by which no man in any nation grows up to manhood (but with which cleaving to him and bringing him into bondage no man ever becomes a true man)—it would seem, I say, as though this natural and acquired selfishness and narrowness were, after all, more than anything else, the *original sin* of human nature. It is, at all events, that without which our humanity in its original simplicity and universality is not developed and differentiated into the particular and individual form. The individualizing element must come forth and assert itself and its claims, but this it is sure to do with an undue emphasis and intensity. The individualizing tendency which is natural and necessary, carries itself to excess, and in that lies the evil, and the wrong, and the sin. It is at this point, and under the temptation that besets us at this initial and feeblest stage of our development, that the sin comes in. It lies not in the individualizing and self-asserting tendency itself, but in the *excess* to which this is permitted to go—it is here that the false and the wrong, the unlovely and the sinful, first make their appearance—at this door they make their entrance. It is for this reason that the unalloyed sweetness, the unsullied brightness of our humanity is seen only in its infancy—before the developing process has begun, and incorporated into it any of the harsh and bitter fruits, any of the baser elements, any of the hard angularities, any of selfish and harsh antagonisms that make the full-grown individuality a thing so false and so full of ugliness that we could almost wish that our nature might forever remain in its infancy, in its undeveloped and characterless simplicity and unsullied purity, so as to reflect upon us nothing but that which it brings with it from heaven, nothing but the pure humanity, radiant with the smiles of the infinite Father, which it still reflects back upon us from its own sweet, unconscious face when it first opens its eyes in wonder upon our faces. There can be no doubt that it was this that so touched the chord of Divine tenderness, and awakened the peculiar thrill of love and delight in the heart of Jesus at the sight of little children, and that caused him to take them in his arms and bless them, and to say: *Suffer the little children to come unto me, and forbid them not, for of such is the kingdom of heaven.* And no doubt herein lies the explanation of the requisition which, with so much emphasis, he lays down upon us: *That except we be converted and become as little children, we can in no wise enter into the kingdom of heaven.* What does he mean, but simply and plainly this: that that simple and universal element in our humanity—the root and principle of all the beautiful and good—which, in the progress of our false development and false lives, becomes overloaded, suppressed and smothered, so that it can scarcely breathe, and so that it can scarcely be said that it lives, must be restored to its original and natural place and power? What he means to say is, that this hard crust of selfishness and custom must be broken up, and the corruptions bred of the strife for self, and self-will, and self-interest, "ill-governed passions, ranklings of despite," be purged out, and that we begin to look upon our fellow-men as our brothers and friends, and not as aliens and enemies—upon ours and theirs, not as mutually antagonistic and exclusive natures and interests, but as really all one in Christ Jesus, all one in virtue of our common humanity and common relationship to the Son of man, the prince and principle and the Saviour of our humanity, where there is neither Greek nor Jew, barbarian Scythian, bond or free, but Christ is all and in all.

I cannot in this connection and as apropos to the momentous topic not handled, but merely alluded to, in passing, above—I mean the strange beauty which attaches itself to the period of infancy—"when God does by himself," without the intervention of the understanding or the reasoning faculties, "seem to converse with our simplicity," and our intellectual power, though undeveloped, seems yet to *be haunted forever by the Eternal mind*—I cannot, I say, forbear quoting a verse from the immortal Ode of Wordsworth, in which the subject is set forth with a depth of imaginative and philosophic insight which finds its equal nowhere in our own language, if, indeed, in any other. Of this poem Coleridge says: To the Ode on the Intimations of Immortality, from recollections of Early Childhood, the poet might have prefixed the lines which Dante addresses to one of his own Canzoni:

> "O lyric song, there will be few, think I,
> Who may thy import understand aright;
> Thou art for them, so arduous, and so high!"

But the Ode was intended for such readers only as had been accustomed to watch the flux and reflux of their inmost nature, to venture at times into the twilight realms of consciousness and to feel a deep interest in modes of inmost being to which they know the attributes of time and space are inapplicable and alien, but which yet cannot be conveyed save in symbols of time and space. For such readers the sense is sufficiently plain, and they will be as little disposed to charge Mr. Wordsworth with believing the Platonic pre-existence in the ordinary interpretation of the words, as I am to believe that Plato himself ever meant or taught it.

To find no contradiction in the union of old and new, to contemplate the *Ancient of Days* with feelings as fresh as if they then sprang forth at his own fiat, this characterizes the minds that feel the riddle of the world and may help to unravel it! To carry on the feelings of childhood into the powers of manhood, to combine the child's sense of wonder and novelty, the appearances which every day for perhaps forty years had rendered familiar

> With sun and moon and stars throughout the year,
> And man and woman.

This is the character and privilege of genius, and one of the marks which distinguish genius from talent. (The Friend, Vol. I., p. 183.) (See Reed's Edition of Wordsworth.)

> " Thou whose exterior semblance doth belie
> Thy soul's immensity:
> Thou best Philosopher, who yet dost keep
> Thy heritage, thou Eye among the blind,
> That deaf and silent read'st the eternal deep,
> Haunted forever by the Eternal Mind,—
> Mighty Prophet! Seer blest!
> On whom those truths do rest,
> Which we are toiling all our lives to find,

In darkness lost, the darkness of the grave;
Thou over whom thy Immortality
Broods like the day, a master o'er a slave,
A presence which is not to be put by;
Then little child, yet glorious in the might
Of heaven-born freedom on thy Being's height,
Why with such earnest pains dost thou provoke
The years to bring the inevitable yoke,
Thus blindly with thy blessedness at strife,
Full soon thy soul shall have her earthly freight,
And *custom* lie upon thee with a weight
Heavy as frost and deep almost as life!"

In the fourth book of the Excursion is another passage to substantially the same purpose, which from identity of thought, and even of language, in one or two striking instances, seems as though it must have been the germ of the Ode, or at least of much that is found in it:

Alas! the endowment of immortal Power,
Is matched unequally with *custom*, *time*
And domineering faculties of sense
In *all*; in most with superadded foes—
Idle temptations—open vanities,
Ephemeral offspring of the unblushing world;
And in the private regions of the mind
Ill-governed passions, ranklings of despite,
Immoderate wishes, pining discontent,
Distress and care. What then remains? To seek
Those helps, for his occasions ever near

Who lacks not will to use them; vows renewed
On the first motion of a holy thought,
Vigils of contemplation; praise and prayer;
A stream, which, from the fountain of the heart
Issuing however feebly, nowhere flows
Without access of unexpected strength.*

---

* By an obvious mistranslation the Apostle Paul is made to represent the sin of the first man, Adam, as the cause of the sin of his posterity, and his death the cause of their death, whereas he teaches no such doctrine. His language (Rom. v. 12) rightly translated, is: Wherefore as by one man sin entered into the world and death by sin (that is, his death by his sin), *even so* death passes upon all men *because all sin.*

Thus the sin of Adam is represented as the *pattern* according to which all men sin. We sin and we die for our sin, not because he did but *as* he did. As Paul in this very connection says that we all sin *after the similitude of Adam's transgression*—the exception mentioned being only an apparent one, and as such, proving the rule (v. 14).

In regard to the interpretation to be given to the description of Adam's sin in the second and third chapters of Genesis, Coleridge (Aids to Reflection, pp. 241–243) writes as follows—I quote, however, but a few of his expressions, and these only because of the very great merit which they seem to me to possess, for the wealth of their learning, the clearness and comprehensiveness of their thought, and the fire of genius by which the whole mass is fused and in which it all glows.

We have the assurance of Bishop Horsley that the Church of England does not demand the literal understanding of the document in the second (from verse 8) and third chapters of Genesis, as a point of faith, or regard a different interpretation as affecting the orthodoxy of the interpreter; divines of the most unexceptionable orthodoxy, and the most averse to the allegorizing of Scripture history in general, having adopted or permitted it in this instance.

And, indeed, no unprejudiced man can pretend to doubt that if in

And it was that this smothered and dying principle of our humanity might be delivered from its bondage and its death, that the Good, in the person of the Incarnate Son of man, came down from heaven *in outward form and fashion as a man*, assumed

---

any work of Eastern origin, he met with trees of life and of knowledge, or talking and conversable snakes :

Inque rei signum serpentem serpere jussum,

he would want no other proof that it was an allegory he was reading, and intended to be understood as such * * * * It cannot be denied that the Mosaic narrative thus interpreted gives a just and faithful exposition of the birth and parentage and successive moments of phenomenal sin, that is, of sin as it reveals itself in time and as an immediate object of consciousness. And in this sense most truly does the Apostle assert that in Adam we all fall. *The first human sinner is the adequate representative of all his successors.* And, with no less truth may it be said that it is the same Adam that falls in every man, and from the same reluctance to abandon the too dear and undivorceable Eve, and the same Eve tempted by the same serpentine and perverted understanding which, formed originally to be the interpreter of the reason and the ministering angel of the spirit, is henceforth sentenced and bound over to the service of the animal nature, its needs and its cravings, dependent on the senses for all its materials, with the world of sense for its appointed sphere: *Upon thy belly shalt thou go, and dust shalt thou eat all the days of thy life.* I have elsewhere shown that as the instinct of the mere intelligence differs in degrees, not in kind and circumstantially, not essentially, from the *vis vitæ*, or vital power in the assimilative and digestive functions of the stomach, and other organs of nutrition, even so the understanding in itself, and distinct from the reason and conscience, differs in degree only from the instinct of the animal. It is still but *a beast of the field*, though more subtle than any beast of the field, and therefore, in its corruption and perversion, *cursed above any*, a pregnant word, etc., etc.

the office of shepherd, guide, guardian and Saviour of our souls. He must, in the discharge of the functions of this office, address himself to that which is simplest and most universal in our souls—that is, to this principle of humanity. It is the only element to which he could address himself, the only one which would be capable of any response to him if he should address himself to it.

It was the almost total death and extinction of this element in the Pharisaic and dominant element among the Jews that led them almost with one consent to reject him, and that made it impossible that they should recognize in him the Good Shepherd, and consequently for him to see in them anything on account of which he could recognize them as his sheep. This is the only and the sovereign test; and he is not timid, nor sparing in his application of it to them. There is nothing in the diabolic rage which the fearless, unequivocal application of it to them excites in them against him that operates in the least to deter him or make him less severe and pointed in his language, But ye believe not because ye are not of my sheep. My sheep hear my voice, and I know them, and they follow me, and I give unto them eternal life, and they shall never perish, neither shall any man pluck them out of my hand. As much as to say, Your hostility against me is in fact hostility against them. To the end that they may be without a shepherd and without a Saviour of their souls from the death that awaits you, you seek to kill me. You may be able to accomplish that, but that will not endanger their welfare, or deprive them of their shepherd. He lives still, all-powerful for their protection, after you have killed him, no less than though you had no power over the life of his body at all. In fact, it is only after he is slain that he enters fully upon his shepherd function and fully develops the power of his office, and becomes to them not prospectively nor by promise merely, but actually and efficaciously the power of an endless life. It is by his laying down his life for his sheep, by means of that voluntary death which he suffers for them, that he fulfills his great promise and accomplishes the great purpose of his ministry.

This function of the Good Shepherd is, therefore, not applicable to nor available for all men alike. It is an office of good *only to those who* (potentially at least) *are good;* to those only, that is, who in their own moral condition and character are susceptible of the good which it is the province and the design of the office to administer. It comes as the minister to our humanity. Where that has perished already, and has no longer any ear to hear or any heart to respond to its offer and purpose of mercy, it has no ministry except one of condemnation and wrath to perform. This is the condemnation, that light has come into the world, and men have loved darkness rather than light, because their deeds are evil. For every one that doeth evil hateth the light, neither cometh to the light lest his deeds should be reproved. But he that doeth truth [that has an element of the love of the true and the good still surviving in his heart, notwithstanding his manifold sins and corruptions] cometh to the light, and thereby makes it manifest that his deeds are wrought in God, [that there is a principle of righteousness at the bottom of them, at least of some of them—the desire and the purpose to come to the light is surely not born of evil, nor is it evil in its nature, but is born of good, and is in its nature good, and leads to good. In that sense *it is wrought* in God, or in other words, it is the fruit of God working in the heart and manifesting himself in the acts of the still unredeemed and struggling man]. (John iii. 19–21.) To the help, to the inarticulate call of this oppressed and struggling principle Christ comes as the good shepherd, to it he becomes the power of an almighty and gracious deliverance, and the principle of an endless life.

In the light of this fact, in the light of the condition of our humanity as thus revealed, we have the explanation of the doctrine of the new birth, and the answer to the question, *Why is it that we must be, and what is it for us to be, born again?* It is simply the reviving to a new life of our humanity which has lain as though it were dead, and which must have died and gone beyond the reach of any reviving influence if it had not been for the voice, and the light, and the power of the truth which comes to its help and restoration in Christ. In order that the soul may truly live, in order that it may hear, and see, and feel—have right understanding, heart and will, and be alive once more unto God, through Jesus Christ our Lord—the humanity within it must experience a radical and effectual quickening. That which is born of the flesh is flesh, and only flesh, that only which is born of the spirit is spirit, that only which is rooted and grounded in a principle of divine love, can have any true human virtue or worth in it. It is only through this spirit of love quickened into life in the heart through the ministration of the Good Shepherd, that we have any true spiritual life, anything of this life of love, or, which is the same thing, anything of the true life of our humanity, for we do not as men truly begin to live until the life of love is begun in us, and this beginning is the result of the new birth.

The truth is, that in regard to the things of the spirit of God, we see with our hearts—in other words, we see nothing rightly until we see it in the light of a loving and a willing heart. The view we take of spiritual things, the light in which they appear to us, will depend entirely upon the sort of affections, in other words, the sort of eyes which we carry in our hearts. We must, therefore, in order that we may catch the true tone and meaning of that which speaks to us in Christ, see with the eyes, feel with the heart of a newly and divinely-quickened humanity. We must have heart, eye, ear, and organs that have been given to us by the spirit living and energizing within. Only those senses and organs that are born of the spirit, that belong to the spirit, only those that are the product of the newly-awakened humanity within us, are truly spiritual, and of course it is by these only that we can discern spiritual things.

The reason why the natural man does not discern spiritual things, and see them in their true light, is that he lacks the proper organ of perception with reference to them. And what is that proper organ? It is the right feeling towards the object. We see in regard to such things by means of our feelings. Our eyes are in our hearts. In other words, *the eyes by which we see spiritual things are the feelings with which we regard them.* The expression may be regarded as a strong one, but it is not too much to say that our sight in respect to things of the spirit is in our feelings—that they are our only organs of vision—nay, our only sources of light. As they are so are our views—so is our understanding and our faith. If our views are wrong, it is because we are blinded to, and prejudiced against, the truth ; either do not see at all or look at things in a wrong light, and from a wrong point of view.

And this furnishes us with a clear interpretation of that pregnant and yet obscure aphorism of our Saviour in respect to the single and the evil eye—The light of the body is the eye. If, therefore, thine eye be single thy whole body shall be full of light, but if thine eye be evil thy whole body shall be full of darkness. If, therefore, the light that is within thee (if the heart that is within be an evil heart that hates the truth) how great is that darkness!

The infidel theory of the religious element and the faith that depends upon it, is that the believer is deluded by his superstitious fancies—that he is the prey of a blind and servile credulity—that he sinks his understanding in his perverted, overwrought and morbid feelings, that by the false colorings and obscuring and distorting mists that come from them, his understanding is blinded and his mind deceived. The Christian theory, on the other hand, is that the eyes of the understanding are enlightened by the power of sanctified feeling, so that not merely with the logical faculties—the dry light of the understanding, but with the very life and vital organs of the soul, the act of correctly seeing and perceiving is performed.

Everything in our moral perceptions, as well as in regard to our views of outward things, depends upon the *point of view*. Love only—as it is the universal and fundamental element in the life of our humanity—gives us that right point with reference to Christ. "You must love him, ere to you he will seem worthy of your love." Love alone gives you the eye by which to see him. As love is the only right moral feeling towards him, so in love alone we have the right point of view from which to regard him. The right point of view in reference to a moral subject is not local or speculative or merely intellectual, it is moral. It consists in the moral character and condition of the man. Every one admits that in order to right views of things, whether internal or external to the mind of the observer, everything depends upon the point from which they are viewed, and that to see anything whatever—whether it relates to the inward or outward senses—we must be rightly situated in regard to it. Now, in respect to spiritual things, character, or the voluntary state of the feelings and affections, constitutes the point of view—it is as the character is—right character constitutes the right, and wrong character the wrong point. Unless, therefore, it is unreasonable to require a right point of view in reference to an object in order to a right view of it, it is perfectly reasonable and logical to require in a man a morally good character, and an unsophisticated and unprejudiced state of the feelings in order to the just apprehension of Christ, and that right character which the right view of him requires consists in love. Love is the fundamental and universal element of the soul's life. The soul has not its true life—it is not too much to say, in the strong language of the apostle, that it is dead in trespasses and in sins—if it have not love as the principle of its life. Does not the apostle say the very same thing, and prescribe a life and a heart of love in order to anything like true spiritual knowledge? Does he not say that we must be *rooted and grounded in love* before we can expect to comprehend—or be in a condition in which it is possible for us to comprehend with all saints, what is the breadth, and length, and depth, and height, and to know the love of Christ which passeth knowledge, that we may be filled with all the fullness of God?

The intelligence which is necessary in order to know, the sensibility which is necessary in order to feel rightly concerning Christ, are all comprehended in love. Without it the soul is, with reference to him, unintelligent, blind, and dead. Love is the understanding, the imagination, and the heart of the soul all combined and acting as one faculty, and all exercised in a single act. With the faculty of love fully developed, and acting in its perfection and power, we need no faculties but what are comprehended in this, and are exercised in it. When it is perfect and has its perfect work—with love existing and operating in its full power within us, *we are perfect and entire, wanting nothing.* Of the truth of this view of the constitution of the human mind with reference to its higher relations and functions, we have a mighty and almost startling confirmation in the inspired representations of the Apostle John (1 John iv. 16), where he virtually declares that God himself is then most justly conceived of when he is regarded as consisting of but a single complex faculty—all his attributes being reducible to the unity of the single faculty of love. *Beloved* (1 John iv. 7, 8), *let us love one another, for love is of God*—what is that but saying, not merely that love comes from God, but that it is *of the nature of God,* and that just so much of love as a man has in him, therefore, just so much of the nature of God. *Every one that loveth is born of God and knoweth God, for God is love.* If we have love we know it, in the only way in which we can truly know anything, and that is by experience, and if we know love, we do in that knowledge know God. If we know love we know God, for God *is* love. He that loveth not consequently knoweth not God—for he hath no means of knowing him. He has not, and cannot have, the experience which involves it, and in and by which alone we have the knowledge of God.

Inspiration in the mind of the Apostle here rises to a height, and assumes an uncompromising boldness and disregard of the conventionalities of human conception and expression that is not with reference to this subject found elsewhere, even in Scripture. It boldly ventures to define to human apprehension the divine being, and to reduce him within the limits of the actual experience and experimental knowledge of man. It says unequivocally, without circumlocution and without a figure, that *God is love*, and conversely with equal directness that *love is God.* If you would know what love is—love in its supreme height and perfection and power, know that it is no other than God himself, and that so much as you have of it, so much of the nature of God has been born and is living in you, and so far your soul has gone in the true knowledge of the nature, and of the mind, and feeling of God. In the feeling and state of mind of which you are conscious when you do truly dwell in the love of your kind, and when that love is the fundamental principle of your own life, and the ruling passion of your heart—in the feeling and state of mind of which you are then conscious, you enter into the consciousness of God himself; in the feeling which you have towards men you enter into the feeling of God, and know him in his feeling, know how he feels towards us, and towards all the objects and interests upon which our love fastens. The Apostle could not say that he that dwelleth in love dwelleth in God and God in him, if love were not virtually God—and love and God convertible terms—or terms which may be used the one for the other without altering the sense. Accordingly, the two propositions God is love and love is God are logical and substantial equivalents. God may be used as the predicate of love with as much propriety as love may be made the comprehensive predicate of God.

All the divine attributes, then, may be ascribed to love as the ultimate substance of being, and when we say that love is the original creative principle out of which the universe sprang, and is ever springing—that it is infinite, eternal, self-existent, almighty, all-wise, all-beneficent and just and good, we declare the same truth and speak with the same propriety as when we say the same things of God—and ascribe the same attributes and agencies to him.

If this be so, if God is love and nothing but what is comprehended in the idea and nature of love, then God does nothing *but love*—or rather does nothing, and has no attribute that does not involve the nature of love in it. All that he does and all that he is, may be regarded as love acting now in one way and now in another, according to the subjects with reference to which he acts—manifesting itself now in one attribute, and now in another according to the nature of the subject or the occasion. The entire agency and manifestation of the divine being may consequently be said to consist in the varied activities that love puts forth, the varied manifestations which it makes of itself, and the manifold forms and directions in which it exerts itself according to the exigencies of the divine agency and administration. There can, therefore, be no such thing as an attribute of justice in God, that is inconsistent with his love. Nay; that does not include love, and is not love acting and manifesting itself with reference to the particular matters and occasions with which justice is concerned. Love will carry out its plans and execute the all-wise and benevolent design in pursuance of which, and for the accomplishment of which, the universe was made. It will feel no pity, and show no mercy towards that which shall put itself in the way of the accomplishment of its purposes. In regard to this the supreme point, love is as inflexible and inexorable as fate—whatever shall resist the purposes of its administration, must either change its position or expect to be consumed by the breath of its mouth, and *destroyed by the brightness of its coming.* The sinner that sins and that perseveres in his sin against all methods and means used for his repentance and reformation, must expect to take the full measure of his sins, he must expect to receive his wages, and there is nothing in the nature of love that can interfere or wish to interfere to prevent his receiving them. Love requires that the purposes of love should be carried out—that which is indifferent to this, or that can prefer any object or interest before this, and not be absolutely inflexible in regard to this, *is not love*—it is some base counterfeit that has usurped its name.

To say that God is love, is to say that whatever vital act he performs is the act of that love which is the fundamental element and principle of his nature.

To say that God is love is to say that every act he performs may be traced to love as its motive and principle—its moving and its final cause. Who can doubt that it is out of love that the creation sprang and is evermore springing? Love, ever-living, ever-acting,—of course never acting without a design—never for the mere sake of acting, but always for the sake of love and for the sake of the good, which it is the very nature of love to seek, and which it cannot act but for the sake of producing and making actual in the condition and experience of the creatures who are the work of its hands. The object of the creation of which love is the cause, is to reveal its own nature and manifest itself to the intelligent universe, the heart and the mind and nature of that divine eternal and creative principle in which is the life of our life—in whom we live and move, and have our being.

In like manner, to say that humanity is love—that man in the uttermost root and principle of his being is love—that every vital and truly human act which a man performs, every act which in virtue and as the expression of his humanity he performs, is the act of love, grows out of it and may be reduced to it, and be regarded as being itself no other than love itself in some or other of its various modes and forms of action and manifestation, according to circumstances, and the manifold demands and occasions of human life.

Here, then, with reference to the natures of God and of man respectively, and their relations to each other, we find ourselves standing on the most fundamental and radical ground. Thought, with reference to God, can go no further than to reduce the idea of him to the unity of the principle and the life of love, and there is no other way by which he can be made intelligible to our minds, or brought home so realizingly to our hearts. In fact, this is the only way in which he can become intelligible to us at all. God can become known and intelligible to us only in the form of life. To reduce him to the unity of an abstract principle is, in fact, to take him entirely out of the sphere of experience, and consequently of rational conception; as Aristotle says, *there is no such thing as a science of the unique*—of the *absolutely abstract and simple.* To represent God, therefore, under this form of conception, is to remove him entirely out of the sphere of objective reality, and of all true and living and realizing thought and knowledge. Hence, in reducing the idea of God to the single conception of love, we reduce him not to the unity of a general and abstract principle, but to the unity of a life. This unity involves distinction and rank of elements and of principles, but it is not an abstraction.

Now love, as life, is matter not of speculation and abstract conception merely, but of experience,—a thing of which we can know nothing except as we feel it, even as life becomes intelligible to us only as it is matter of personal consciousness.

If, then, God is love and love is life, and to be known only so far and in the degree in which it is felt by us, it follows, of necessity, that God becomes known to us only in our feelings, and that the heart is the only organ of the true knowledge of God. He is no object of the merely speculative understanding any more than of the outward and bodily senses. He is the object of the inward, moral sense, and of spiritual perception only.

In the inner, spiritual sense, therefore, or, in other words, in the moral condition or state of the heart we have our only just point of view with reference to the knowledge of God. If our feelings towards him are right, that is, if we love him, then according to the strength and purity of our love *we see him as he is*, and, as our love increases in purity and strength, our ideas become more and more clear, our faith more and more realizing, until in virtue of its love the soul comes to stand face to face with its blessed and glorious Author. This makes clear the meaning of the Apostle, and reveals to us the philosophy of the soul's knowledge of God, as he sets it forth in the memorable words (1 John iii. 12): *Beloved, now are we the sons of God, and it doth not yet appear what we shall be, but we know that when he shall appear, we shall be like him, for we shall see him as he is.* Our seeing him as he is, he makes to depend upon our being like him, and our being like him consists in our love, for love is of the very nature of God. When, therefore, we become filled with his love, we are filled with his nature—we are full of that which is of his very nature, and so are changed into his very image and likeness through the transforming power of love. As Paul says, by beholding, as in a glass, the glory of the Lord, we are changed into the same image from one degree of conformity to another. When this love becomes the life and the vital organ of the soul, when it becomes, at once, the eye with which it sees, the mind and the heart with which it feels and perceives and knows, then the true union between God and man is accomplished, and the most blessed and glorious of all consummations is reached. Then the humanity, as it is in man, beholds its own divine counterpart and original, as it is in the Son of Man. Then the humanity, as it is in the finite image, stands face to face with itself as it is in its own divine original. Humanity, as it is in the members, then finds itself standing face to face with itself as it is in its own fountain-head. It has the most blissful and the most enrapturing and the most soul-transforming of all sights; not another humanity outside of, and yet co-ordinate with and like itself, as we stand in relation to each other, but that humanity which is itself, its own counterpart, the eternal source out of which it has sprung, and in which it lives, and moves, and has its being, and which, conversely, lives, and moves, and has its being in it.

Let it be inquired whether there is any delight which the soul can experience, any perfection of which it can be the subject which can come into any comparison with, or at all resemble, or take the place of this, which the soul has, in thus living the life of love? What joy can be compared to that which the soul feels when thus by loving and dwelling in love it dwelleth in God and God in it? If, then, the life of love is a life in God, must it not, so far as it is such, and so far as love is its vital principle, be an absolutely pure, and blessed, and Godlike life? Is not our ideal of a perfect and blessed humanity fully realized in the experiences and attributes of such a life as this? Not until we come to look upon the matter in this light, and see in Christ the living and eternal spring of our humanity and of our joy, can we have any proper conception of the joy with which the soul beholds its Redeemer. Until then we can have no idea of the depth and the satisfying sweetness of meaning expressed in the title which, with reference to his relations to the soul's satisfaction and salvation, he gives to himself—that of the *Good Shepherd.* It is not as a kind benefactor, outside of us, exercising care and protection over us, as a parent over a child, as a paternal and just and wise ruler over his subjects, or a magistrate over the people whom he rules only to serve, not for the sake of being ministered unto by them, but for the sake of ministering to them—making himself their servant rather than them his. It is not as such merely that we are to conceive of Christ in his administration of the office of the Good Shepherd towards us. It is not as an outward thing that we are to conceive of his administration as the shepherd and bishop of our souls. The ministration of love and care which he performs towards us is primarily an inward one,—like that of the fountain to the stream, or that of the vine to the branch, which groweth out of it and has its life and fruitfulness in it.

His office is indeed to be the minister of eternal

life and peace to our souls, but this office he can administer to us in no other way than by himself becoming the fountain-head and perpetual and exhaustless spring of that life and peace by his own actual indwelling within us, and thus becoming, not indeed our life, not making our life *identical* with his—for that would be no personal privilege to us—it would only destroy our personality and capacity of personal enjoyment by absorbing our persons in his own.

There could be no blessedness to us in a life or in a blessedness which is not our own; but he becomes life to us by giving and preserving to each of us out of his own life, as the fountain-head, a life of our own, and thus himself becoming the life of that life which is truly our own, and is, therefore, sweet to us. It is thus, in administering his own life to us, as the source and principle of our lives, and making it the everlasting and holy spring of our lives, and of all the holiness, and all the joy we have in our lives, that he discharges towards us the office of the Good Shepherd.

It is in this that the unique and peculiar character of his shepherdship consists. It is in this respect that his office differs not in degree only, but in kind also, from any office or ministry which men can discharge towards each other; I mean in the relation which the administrator sustains to that which he administers—*the offerer to that which he has to offer.* Among men, and within the earthly sanctuary or sphere of service and offering, the things which they who enter into that sanctuary bring as offerings are one thing; but the offerers or high-priests themselves are another, the priest and his offering, the magistrate and the justice that he administers, are not identical. But in the case of this high-priesthood of the Good Shepherd, the offerer and that which he offers, the shepherd and that which he administers to his sheep, are one and the same thing. Having nothing else to offer, there being in the universe nothing else which, in the nature of the case, could constitute an acceptable, that is, an effectual, life-giving and soul-saving offering, he *offers himself.* By so much, and for this reason, was Jesus made the surety of a better covenant, established upon better promises. And they truly were many priests, because they were not suffered to continue by reason of death—but this great high-priest, who is not made after the law of a carnal commandment, but after the power of an endless life,—this high-priest, because he continueth ever, hath an unchangeable priesthood, for every high-priest is ordained to offer gifts and sacrifices; *wherefore it is of necessity that this man have some-*

what also to offer. But, seeing that the gift which he has to bring into the sanctuary as his offering for us is no other than eternal life to our souls, and seeing that he himself, the offerer, is that eternal life which he comes to give, it is plain that if he is to give us eternal life, he must give it in himself, that is, by giving himself for us. He must himself be not only the sacrificer, but the sacrifice. *But Christ, being come a high-priest of good things to come by a greater and more perfect tabernacle* not made with hands, neither by the blood of goats and calves, but *by his own blood*, he entered in once into the holy place, having thereby to obtain, and obtaining, eternal redemption for us.

This is the record that God hath given us eternal life, and that this Life is in his Son. He, therefore, that hath the Son hath Life, and he that hath not the Son of God hath not Life. All of which makes it very plain and certain that the good-shepherd and great high-priest of our souls can in no other way administer the good things which have been committed to him for his people, than by making himself the matter of the gift which he has to bestow—of the offering which he has to bring—as this life, this good thing, which God has to administer to us through him, is *in himself*, he can in no other way administer it than by making himself at once the minister and the thing administered, at once the great high-priest, and the supreme and all-perfect, and all-sufficient sacrifice which he brings.

The only effectual sacrifice which he can offer for us is himself; and the only way in which he can offer it is by the sacrifice of himself.

He enters into the sanctuary, therefore, not with the blood of beasts, but with his own blood, which, being interpreted, means that through the suffering and self-sacrificing ministry which, in the flesh, he performs for us, he makes his life ours, or the means of life to us, or rather makes the eternal life which is in him the principle of an immortal and blessed life to us. He imparts his own life to us in such a way that he does not thereby himself cease to live, but makes his own life, while he keeps and preserves it to himself, the everlasting principle and spring of life to us.

The spectacle of his life and of his death, when properly reviewed and appreciated by us, produces, through the superadded ministration of the Holy Spirit, a moral effect upon our consciences and our hearts, imparts a light, and fastens convictions and impressions upon us that cannot be resisted or shaken off, and that in the end become absolutely subduing and transforming in their effect upon our souls. It is thus that he lays down his life for his sheep, and thus that he gives unto them eternal life. Through the moral effect of his passion the humanity within them is born again, and thus is begotten again in them that new life of humanity of which he is the principle, the high-priest, and administrator. And, having imparted the principle, he secures us in the possession of it and makes it sure that we shall never perish, nor any power of hostility or hatred to him or to us, whether in this world or that which is to come, pluck us out of his hand.

How does he accomplish this? I answer, by putting the treasure within us—into our very mind and heart, and thus placing it forever beyond the reach of any will or any power but his and our own. He puts it into our own hands in such a way as to make us, in regard to the secure possession of it, independent of any power or will but our own. And, besides, the gift is of such a nature that it must, under all circumstances, be esteemed and valued by us as absolutely above all price. And it is made to depend entirely upon the soul's voluntary choice and consent whether it will part with it or not. The life which it enjoys in it is one of perfect blessedness; and can anything be conceived of that could prevail upon the soul once in the possession and enjoyment of it to make it willing to part with it? God, on his part, cannot fail. There is no power in the universe that can compel or induce him to withdraw his everlasting and almighty love and protection from the soul that loves him. What shall we, then, say to these things? If God be for us, who can be against us? He that spared not his own Son, but delivered him up for us all, how shall he not with him also freely give us all things? Who shall lay anything to the charge of God's elect?

It is God that justifieth. Who is he that condemneth? It is Christ that died, yea, rather, that is risen again, who is even at the right hand of God, who also maketh intercession for us.

It is Christ that lives; and because he lives, and lives in us as the sustaining principle of our life, we shall live also. Our immortality rests upon the same securities as those which make his life an eternal certainty.

V.

THE GIST OF THE CONTROVERSY:

OR,

A plain word with Prof. Tyndall on the question of the Origin of Life.

IT seems to me that the Professor, in his late remarkable deliverance upon this subject, deserves the credit of having spoken plainly, and presented the issue between science and religion with great clearness and force—if they are, indeed, at issue at all, and that is indeed science, rightly so called, which, under that name, he arrays against the universal religious instinct of mankind. We, however, deny that that which he thus, on this great and fundamental question, arrays against the instincts of religion is science at all, and maintain that his position is in fact, and can easily be shown to be, as unscientific as it is atheistic.

But if they were at issue, as he boldly claims, and there were no alternative but to side with the one against the other—the fundamental position of the one being irreconcilable with that of the other—

then the issue between them appears to be fairly presented. And it is doubtless well that it is so, if the question is to come up and be seriously debated at all. In the end, no harm, but rather advantage, must come to the truth from the presentation, rash and dangerous as it may at first seem. If the result shall be to make more clear to the Christian mind the strength of the argument upon which its cause and its faith rest, we shall have occasion to rejoice that the issue has been presented and the discussion provoked.

As he presents the case, the difference between science and religion, with reference to the question of the origin of the organic universe, or as to the first principle out of which it springs, is that science finds all that is necessary to account for the actual world in the primordial atoms or molecules of Democritus and Epicurus.

Upon the hypothesis of these original and ultimate atoms science bases the fact of the existing universe of life and being. The words in which the Professor lays down his great thesis are memorable: "*Prolonging the vision backward across the line of experimental evidence, we find in matter the promise and the potency of every form and quality of life.*"

The doctrine, then, is that out of this hypothetical principle or ground, which he calls matter, and out of these ultimate molecules or atoms, and the inorganic forces inherent in them, all the species and forms, all the grades and orders, all the dependencies and interdependencies of the actual living universe spring. Science excludes and repudiates every other postulate or principle, and says: If these are not God, then there is no God, for there is no God but these; *final causes*, consequently, there are none in the universe, nor are any needed. The universe is what it is without design, and as the result of the unconscious blind force of inorganic, lifeless matter.

Matter acting from its own inherent necessity of acting, and without any end in view, has produced this which we see, and are, and which we call the universe. The plain declaration of this so-called science is that in this—in this blind, unconscious force of hypothetical atoms—we have all that we want—all that reason can ask for in order to account for the universe as it is. All that there is in the creation we have without any God, and without the necessity of presupposing the existence of any, except what is furnished us in this hypothesis of matter. This appears to be a fair statement of the position of science on this question, as represented by Prof. Tyndall and his school.

The position of religion, on the contrary, is that

the atoms, even admitting their existence (though of this Prof. Tyndall admits there is no evidence), are not sufficient to account for the facts in the case as both parties admit them to be. She insists that in order to account for the living creation a creative, intelligent, and benevolent principle is required; that nothing short of such a principle can account for the facts as we find them, for the creation as it is.

The first principle must, as is agreed on all hands, be a creative and producing power; whether voluntarily or consciously or not, it must be producing; and must produce from itself, and be self-moved in production. Science, according to Prof. T., claims that the atoms are such a principle; that out of the inherent forces and tendencies wrapped up in them, and constituting their nature and substance, all the forms and species of living beings spring forth as spontaneous and necessary productions. Spontaneity, necessary self-activity, and self-existence it must ascribe to these atoms if they are ultimate, as they are claimed to be, in the creation, and *all things were made by them, and without them was not anything made that was made*, and they are to have the place in the atheistic cosmogony which the Eternal Word has in the Christian.

But intelligent and self-conscious design in acting

it denies to them. In other words, it assigns to the creation these atoms as its moving or producing cause, but denies to it any such thing as a final cause altogether.

But the facts of the creation imply, not a producing cause merely, but a final cause also. To account for the universe as it is, not a cause only but an intelligent and designing cause, is required; that is, a cause not only acting and producing, but acting and producing with intelligent and wise design. Moreover, to account for the universe as it is, not intelligence only, but benevolence also is required in the cause that produced it, and the effect of whose productive energy it is.

For it is just as evident that the design of the universe is a good design, that is, a design prompted by infinite wisdom and goodness, as that there is any design in it at all, and design, that is, adaptation of means to ends in it, is just as evident as that it exists at all. So that the wisdom and benevolence are just as manifest as the power and the intelligence. The atoms, therefore, being merely blind force, do not account for the facts. He does not deny, he doubtless admits, the evidence of intelligence, or of something looking like, and suggesting intelligence, and of something looking like an all-wise and benevolent end in the creation, and yet he insists that there is in reality no such thing, but that the whole is sprung out of a force to which no such attributes as wisdom or benevolence can be ascribed.

It is a gross absurdity. If science, as antagonistic to religion, has nothing better than this to offer, it had better give up the contest, or else be, for the present, a little more modest in its pretensions.

I do not think that intelligent Christians themselves are generally aware of the strength of the argument on which their cause rests. I do not think they are aware how plainly and forcibly the Scripture puts it. It is sometimes said, and too generally admitted, that the Scriptures have no philosophy of their own; that they deal mainly in general and arbitrary assertions and implications in the truth of which they require us to believe, asking no questions as to the rational or philosophic grounds upon which they are based. But let us see what the Apostle John has to say upon this very subject. Let us see what his idea of God is. For plainly he has an idea of him, and does not hesitate in very plain and positive terms to declare what it is. And let us see whether there be philosophy, or mere vague implication and assertion in his position, or not. It seems to me that there is not only philosophy but argument in it; argument addressed to the reason as well as the religion of man. He says *that God is love, and that he that dwelleth in love dwelleth in God, and God in Him!* What is that but plainly and unequivocally declaring that love is God? We put it, then, to the Professor and his school: Do you deny the reality in human experience of any such thing as the love of which the Apostle here speaks, and which he says is God? Do you deny that love in the broad and fundamental sense in which John uses the word is an essential element in the life of the soul? If you believe in any such thing as the life of the soul in distinction from that of the body you must believe that that life has elements, and that love is one of them, and the most fundamental one.

Now, then, it remains only to ask for a definition of love. We have seen that it exists as an element of human consciousness and experience. That it is no hypothesis, but a *fact*, lying, not on the "*other*," but on *this*, side "*the line* of experimental evidence," and strictly within the legitimate domain of experience and science. We ask, then, in regard to it, Is it not a cause, a principle, a force in life, and in character, and wherever it appears? And is it not more than this? Is it not also an intelligent and benevolent cause or force? You will admit that love exists, and that where it exists it involves these elements: productive force, intelligence, and a design of good, in all that it does; that there cannot be such a thing as a love that is without productive, self-active force, unintelligent or malevolent. An inert, unintelligent, or malevolent love is simply a contradiction in terms. That which knows nothing and does nothing and designs nothing can have no will of its own, and can therefore be neither benevolent or malevolent—can wish or design neither that which is good nor that which is evil. Love, if it means anything, means good-will, acting freely with a wise and intelligent design. Now the apostle says, that he that dwells in that principle, that is, the man who, in all that he does, is actuated by it, dwells in God and God in him, and thus he makes and intends to make love to be but another term for God. We have only to endow love thus understood with infinite attributes and place it at the head of the creation as its producing and final cause, to have the Christian idea of God. According to the philosophy of Christianity, therefore, as expounded by the Apostle John, not only is God infinite and eternal love, but infinite and eternal love is God. He that denies the existence of the God of Christianity, denies that there is any such thing as this love, and claims that he can account for all the life and all the good there is in the universe, all the harmony, and all the beauty, all the happiness that sentient and intelligent creatures enjoy, without supposing love to have anything at all to do with the work of creation.

He claims that a producing cause, without any love, or intelligence, or life in it is sufficient to account for all the life, all the love, all the well-being, and all the happiness there is in the universe. This is the sublime conclusion to which science, divorced from religion, has at last come. This we are told is the last and greatest of its achievements thus far. What may we not expect that it will do in the future! To sum up in one word, the Christian philosophy makes love to be the origin of the creation, and says that all things were made by it, and that without it was not anything made that was made. The infidel philosophy enthrones matter, and makes all the life, and all the love, and all the mind there is in the universe the product of that. The one says *love*, the other says *matter*, is God.

www.ingramcontent.com/pod-product-compliance
Lightning Source LLC
LaVergne TN
LVHW011219110826
845150LV00006B/1483

* 9 7 8 1 4 2 5 5 1 6 3 0 7 *